TYPEWRITING DRILLS FOR SPEED AND ACCURACY

Brenga Muriel Dudley
1725-A. newhall Street
San Francisco. CA. 94124
826-4096

FOURTH EDITION

JOHN L. ROWE, Ed.D.
Late Chairman
Business and Vocational Education
University of North Dakota

FABORN ETIER, Ed.D.
Associate Professor
Division of Office Administration
and Business Education
The University of Texas at Austin

GREGG DIVISION/McGRAW-HILL BOOK COMPANY
New York   St. Louis   Dallas   San Francisco
Auckland   Bogotá   Düsseldorf   Johannesburg
London   Madrid   Mexico   Montreal
New Delhi   Panama   Paris   São Paulo
Singapore   Sydney   Tokyo   Toronto

Sponsoring Editor: **Audrey Schmidt Rubin**
Senior Editing Manager: **Elizabeth Huffman**
Editing Supervisor: **Barbara Brooks**
Production Manager: **Gary Whitcraft**
Designer: **Bill Frost**

Library of Congress Cataloging in Publication Data

Rowe, John L
  Typewriting drills for speed and accuracy.

  Published in 1952 under title: Typewriting for speed and accuracy.
  Includes index.
  1. Typewriting.   I. Etier, Faborn, joint author.
II. Title.
Z49.R88   1977   652.3   76-50096
ISBN 0-07-054151-5

CONTENTS

PREFACE

Typewriting Drills for Speed and Accuracy, Fourth Edition, provides practice materials designed to help any typist improve his or her speed and accuracy—both rapidly and significantly— whether practicing alone or in a group, whether a beginner or an expert.

The most promising development in basic typing instruction has been refinement of the principle of selective practice: a typist will improve most rapidly by focusing, or pinpointing, practice primarily on what he or she needs most to improve. *Typewriting Drills for Speed and Accuracy* has been a pioneer in this con-cept, providing alternative drills for speed practice and accuracy practice and periodic tests, by means of which the learner knows which drills to pursue. In this edition, each individual practice session, or Skill Drive, provides alternative drills for speed practice and a pretest (Inventory), by means of which the student learns what to practice next.

Selective practice directs the learner to the kinds of drills that will be most helpful for the area in which improvement is needed. Selective practice reduces the risk of negative practice by keeping the typist from spending too much time on the wrong kind of drill—accuracy drills, for example, when a speed gain is needed, and vice versa. Selective practice involves two kinds of alternatives: alternative materials and alternative prac-tice procedures. *Both* are incorporated in this book.

The materials in this book have been organized to ensure specific improvement impact for all its drills. This edition con-tains an in-depth presentation of almost every kind of type-writing drill there is, and each drill occurs at the point where, in balance with others, it is most likely to be helpful.

Special thanks are due the many teachers and graduate stu-dents whose classroom experimentation provided the founda-tions on which the standards in this book are based.

HOW TO USE THIS BOOK

THE PLAN IN GENERAL

This book has a built-in design to help you improve your typing speed and accuracy *together*—each in balance with the other— so that there is no chance of damaging one by overemphasizing the other.

If you wish, you can type right through the book, doing every drill. Or you can type only the speed drills (if your need for speed is that urgent) or only the accuracy drills (if your need for greater accuracy is overwhelming). But if you wish to make the most of all that is in this book—if you want to boost both speed and accuracy—then you are urged to follow the plan around which this book is designed.

The design involves practicing a series of period-length Skill Drives. Note the term *period-length.* The plan is not for 5 minutes yesterday, 15 minutes today, 10 minutes tomorrow; that kind of practice schedule never made an expert of anyone! Rather, this plan is for full-fledged, all-out efforts of 40 or 50 minutes of intensive *drive, drive, drive* for improvement.

Each Skill Drive, or lesson, consists of three pages: (1) an Inventory test to define your practice goal for the period, (2) one page of speed drills, and (3) one page of accuracy drills. There is a Progress Test after every three Skill Drives to measure the impact of your practice.

THE INVENTORY EFFORT

Practice needs change as you climb the skill ladder. One day you may need to emphasize speed; the next day you may need to continue stressing speed, or you may need to devote extra attention to accuracy. It is important that you know the right goal, for it is very wasteful (and perhaps self-defeating) to em-phasize the wrong goal. If you *should* push for accuracy but stress speed instead, for example, your push for speed could injure or impede your accuracy improvement. It is essential that you select your practice correctly. How do you know which goal is right? The Inventory test will tell you.

The Inventory test is either a 3- or a 5-minute timed writing on paragraph copy (see page 7 for an example). The goal for each Skill Drive, or class period, is determined by your speed and error scores on the Inventory. In general, your goal should be for speed when your errors are within bounds but for accuracy when your errors are excessive.

The table below indicates the appropriate relation between speed and errors. For example, suppose your speed on a 3-minute writing is 34 words a minute. Referring to the first line of the table, you find the 30–39 span, within which your 34 score falls. Looking at the two lines below the 30–39 panel, you see that an error score up to 5 means you should stress speed (Sp) in the drive and an error score of 6 or more means you should stress accuracy (Ac). (The principle is the same on 5-minute timings.)

3 MINUTES	If your 3-minute speed is	20–29		30–39		40–49		50–59		60–69		70–up	
	And your error score is	to 6	7 up	to 5	6 up	to 4	5 up	to 3	4 up	to 2	3 up	1	2 up
	Your practice goal should be for	Sp	Ac	Sp	Ac	Sp	Ac	Sp	Ac	Sp	Ac	Sp	Ac

5 MINUTES	If your 5-minute speed is	20–29		30–39		40–49		50–59		60–69		70–up	
	And your error score is	to 7	8 up	to 6	7 up	to 5	6 up	to 4	5 up	to 3	4 up	to 2	3 up
	Your practice goal should be for	Sp	Ac	Sp	Ac	Sp	Ac	Sp	Ac	Sp	Ac	Sp	Ac

These "goal tables," explained above, appear on each Inventory page

```
rid sit rod sir the sod row lay man ham
rid sit rod sir the sod row lay man ham
rid sit rod sir the sod row lay man ham

able buff clam dock exit flex glad hold
able buff clam dock exit flex glad hold
able buff clam dock exit flex glad hold

under valve water young along brick spy
under valve water young along brick spy
under valve water young along brick spy
```

```
rid sit rod sir the sod row lay man ham
able buff clam dock exit flex glad hold
under valve water young along brick spy

rid sit rod sir the sod row lay man ham
able buff clam dock exit flex glad hold
under valve water young along brick spy

rid sit rod sir the sod row lay man ham
able buff clam dock exit flex glad hold
under valve water young along brick spy
```

Example A: *Use the line-repetition pattern when your goal is speed.*

Example B: *Use the group-repetition pattern when your goal is accuracy.*

IMPROVEMENT PRACTICE

After you define your practice goal, go on to the speed drills on the second page of the Skill Drive (page 8, for example) and then the accuracy drills on the third page (page 9, for example). Note that you should practice *all* the drills on *both* pages, no matter what your goal is; but the repetition pattern and the number of repetitions differ, depending on the goal.

Repetition Pattern. As illustrated above, any set of drills may be practiced in two different patterns of repetition: by single lines (Example *A*) and by groups of lines (Example *B*). Use the *line*-repetition pattern on all lines when your goal is speed; use the *group*-repetition pattern on all lines when your goal is accuracy.

Number of Repetitions. The drills that correspond to your goal for the period should be typed three times; the others should be typed twice. A reminder to this effect appears at the top of each drill page.

Two Examples. If you type 34 words a minute for 5 minutes with 4 errors, the goal table shows that you should concentrate on speed building by typing *each line* of the speed drills three times, and then typing each accuracy drill line twice.

If you type 52 words a minute for 5 minutes with 5 errors, your goal is accuracy. Use the group-repetition pattern, and type the speed drills twice. Then type each group of accuracy drills three times.

If you have time, repeat the Inventory Test to measure your improvement or repeat the speed or accuracy drills, depending on your goal.

PROGRESS TESTS

After every three Skill Drives there is a full-page selection (page 10, for example) for you to use as a checkup on your progress. Take two 3- or 5-minute writings on this test copy, and average your two speed scores and two error scores. By comparing the averages on successive Progress Tests, you should find marked improvement. If you do not note such progress, ask your teacher to observe you closely and to confirm that you are following all the directions.

You will find it helpful to record your daily Inventory timed writing scores. However, it is *essential* that you keep a record of your Progress Test scores, since they tell you how much progress you are making and alert you to the need for additional coaching if you do not make the progress that you should make.

SPEED

ACCURACY

1-A   WARMUP   Line—60 • Spacing—1 • Each Line 3 Times

		WORDS
1	a ; s l d k f j g h f j d k s l a ; a ; s l d k f j g h f j	12
2	and hit lax new owl tea rub yak war sac oil has auk jug fey	24
3	The sharp knife and ax cut the hay and ivy with great ease.	36

1-B   INVENTORY   Tab—5 • Spacing—2 • Minutes—3 or 5

4	Do not expect that success in your job will come quickly or easily.		15
	On the contrary, you will have to work hard for it. Promotion does not		29
	come from hard work alone; more often, it is given because of the ease		43
	with which the difficult task is accomplished. In order to get ahead, you		58
	must grow in value. A good employee will need to grow mentally every		72
	day. When you have learned all you can about your job and your firm,		86
	do not be satisfied; but widen your interests and set your sights on new		101
	goals. You can learn new knowledge and skills by attending night classes		116
	and by acquiring useful hobbies. Be prepared for the next step, and keep		131
	your eyes on the goal just ahead.		139
5	Study the ways of your employer, learn how he or she wishes	13	152
	things to be done, and then do your best to please your employer by	27	166
	performing your tasks in the way he or she prefers. Demonstrate willing-	41	180
	ness to do more than is expected of you. Accept petty annoyances	54	193
	cheerfully. Take advantage of the increased burden of added duties to	69	208
	demonstrate your own skill and reserve powers.	78	217
6	Business respects and rewards leadership. The leader must have	14	231
	vision, tact, and earnestness and must be able to make decisions quickly	28	245
	and correctly. The leader not only will create, plan, and develop ideas	43	260
	but will also know the time and the place for them to be put into action.	58	275
	It is no simple task to be a leader. Study your strong points, and use	72	289
	them to advantage.	76	293

| 1 | 2 | 3 | 4 | 5 | 6 | 7 | 8 | 9 | 10 | 11 | 12 | 13 | 14 | 5.61/1.39*

1-C   SELECT PRACTICE GOAL   Base It on 1-B Writing

3 MINUTES	If your 3-minute speed is	20–29		30–39		40–49		50–59		60–69		70–up	
	And your error score is	to 6	7 up	to 5	6 up	to 4	5 up	to 3	4 up	to 2	3 up	1	2 up
	Your practice goal should be for	Sp	Ac	Sp	Ac	Sp	Ac	Sp	Ac	Sp	Ac	Sp	Ac

5 MINUTES	If your 5-minute speed is	20–29		30–39		40–49		50–59		60–69		70–up	
	And your error score is	to 7	8 up	to 6	7 up	to 5	6 up	to 4	5 up	to 3	4 up	to 2	3 up
	Your practice goal should be for	Sp	Ac	Sp	Ac	Sp	Ac	Sp	Ac	Sp	Ac	Sp	Ac

* Average strokes per word, 5.61/Average syllables per word, 1.39

To measure the effectiveness of your practice in
Skill Drives 25, 26, and 27 take two 5-minute
timed writings and average your speed and error scores.

Line—60 • Tab—5 • Spacing—2

WORDS

1   Our new plant, which will be open to the general public soon,   12
covers three acres of land and is located near the lake. We feel that we   27
have the largest display of boats found in the United States. We have   41
boats of every conceivable size, description, and price. Whether your   56
preference is a yacht, sailboat, canoe, or cabin cruiser, we have one that   71
we are sure will please you and your family.   80

2   You may have been hesitant about owning a boat because of the   13   93
problem of transporting it cross-country. This is no longer a problem. A   28   108
new boat, which has just been introduced to the public for the first time   43   123
this year, is extremely light in weight and can be transported on the top   58   138
of your car without any damage to the car. It can be assembled   71   151
in fifteen minutes for a water cruiser and then converted at night into a   86   166
family tent that accommodates four adults.   94   174

3   If you are particularly fond of sailing, check our complete line of   15   189
sailboats. You will be delighted by the light weight and the wide choice   28   202
of deck and sail colors available.   36   210

4   Houseboats are becoming more and more popular each year.   13   223
Families are now spending weeks and even months on houseboats, where   26   236
they have the conveniences of home plus the fun and excitement of the   40   250
water. Imagine the fun of diving into a huge lake of water for an early   55   265
morning dip, or fishing from the porch of the houseboat.   67   277

5   Our large houseboat will accommodate eight adults. It includes a   14   291
living room with twin sofas—which may be converted into double beds—   28   305
and a dinette. Some of the models have a separate stateroom and bath.   43   320
You will be pleasantly surprised by the smooth cruising of the new   56   333
houseboats.   58   335

|1 |2 |3 |4 |5 |6 |7 |8 |9 |10 |11 |12 |13 |14   5.66/1.42

1-D SPEED BUILDERS

Line—60 • Spacing—1

EASY WORD RHYTHMS

WORDS

7	aid bob cob doe elf fit gum hem irk jet key lob man nay oak	12
8	maid name odor pair quiz rout site tick uric vial when yore	24
9	aisle bible chaos digit amend field giant hairy ivory Japan	36

WORD PATTERNS

10	the theater theirs theism theory theft therm them they then	12
11	ter banister minister adapter plaster taunter filter master	24
12	tea teacupful teamster tearful teaches teasel teak tear tea	36

STROKING

13	Over and over again they tried harder and harder to finish.	12
14	The dogs ran and ran on the path that went round and round.	24
15	They looked all over and over and made change after change.	36

PHRASING

16	for her for him for she for his for the for its for now for	12
17	the ant the arm the bus the cow the dog the fox the pet the	24
18	and hoe and nip and pay and rob and tap and wed and win and	36

SPEED SENTENCES

19	They must now go to the class for the first time this year.	12
20	The child liked to see the cats and dogs play and have fun.	24
21	We should go to the lakes and catch some fish for our meal.	36

SPACE BAR

22	garment adopt dairy birth maple never stir odor aim hid mow	12
23	senator weight clip helps light rigid trek clip air pen rod	24
24	fragile tempt empty inlay quite opera unit name cry won two	36

| 1 | 2 | 3 | 4 | 5 | 6 | 7 | 8 | 9 | 10 | 11 | 12 |

27-E   ACCURACY BUILDERS   Line—60 • Spacing—1

KEYBOARD REVIEW   WORDS

25   The jacket in question had sixty, woven, hazel—soft strips.   12
26   Vicky placed a dozen gold jugs from Iraq on the waxy table.   24
27   Morning express trains leave at 7:02, 7:32, 7:43, and 7:57.   36

WORD PATTERNS

28   ses parentheses compressing premises stressed recess theses   12
29   pan panchromatic pandemonium pantomime panhandle panic pane   24
30   ony symphony ceremony lemony felony colony agony irony pony   36

NUMBERS AND SYMBOLS

31   $65.19 $51.96 $52.19 $17.18 $20.19 $70.60 $13.20 $71.44 $15   12
32   (1,637) (1,401) (1,834) (1,916) (1,876) (1,976) (1,412) (5)   24
33   1,112# 1,776# 1,913# 1,761# 8,831# 9,961# 7,633# 5,031# 14#   36

WORDS AND PHRASES

34   reference advantage question contents editions books should   12
35   the library, write for new pamphlets, and keep the files in   24
36   and postal guides, trade books, and even an etiquette book.   36

CONCENTRATION: TYPE EACH LINE BACKWARDS

37   .pu gnikool fo tibah eht kaerb ot yaw a si sdrawkcab gnipyT   12
38   .tuo sdrow evael netfo uoy fi uoy rof ecitcarp doog si sihT   24
39   Tom. of aid the to come to men good all for time the is Now   36

SYMBOL SENTENCES

40   Sell 125 shares of XYZ Steel at $32; buy it back at $26.50.   12
41   I was charged as follows: (a) $6.50; (b) $8.25; (c) $9.25.   24
42   We want the sign to read as follows: Fong & Garcia & Kane.   36
        |1 |2 |3 |4 |5 |6 |7 |8 |9 |10 |11 |12

1-E   ACCURACY BUILDERS

Line—60 • Spacing—1

ALPHABET-REVIEW RHYTHMS

		WORDS
25	hag nip jar nak lye wet set elm fit cat que zip nix bad vow	12
26	gym ewe job kit tax zig spy quo bud can far vag lag hay arc	24
27	ale fly cut qui pad tie wax yew bug zoa for ham joy kin vas	36

CAPITALS

28	Abi Bab Col Day Eli Fae Gil Hal Ida Joy Ken Lia Mae Nan Oda	12
29	Abra Bart Cara Dale Ebba Fred Gail Hank Ione John Katy Lane	24
30	Agnes Barry Carin Daryl Edith Felix Glory Heath Irene James	36

ALPHABET-REVIEW SENTENCES: A THROUGH C

31	Ample accusations are always apparent among all applicants.	12
32	Bib boats brought beautiful blooming bouquets by black bag.	24
33	Cowboys can corral carefully chosen cattle conscientiously.	36

PHRASES AND WORDS

34	which was made came up with about the work for a few it can	12
35	job such doing secure aspects benefits resources attempting	24
36	you can to seek above all you have added to secure the same	36

CONCENTRATION

37	fad fan far fat gab gad gag gam gap gar gas gat had ham hat	12
38	hem hen hew hex hey hid hie hip hit hob hod hoe hog hop hot	24
39	hud hue hug hum hut jab jam jar jaw jet jib jig job jot joy	36

REINFORCEMENT

40	Most students finished their work so that the teacher would	12
41	know that they understood what was to be done. The job was	24
42	difficult, and the teacher was happy with the final result.	36

|1 |2 |3 |4 |5 |6 |7 |8 |9 |10 |11 |12

27-D · SPEED BUILDERS

Line—60 • Spacing—1

SYMBOL FLUENCY: BASIC REACHES

WORDS

7   f5%bf j6_nj f4$vf j7&mj d3#cd k8',k s2"xs l9(.l ;0)/; ;0);   12

8   f%bf j_nj f$vf j&mj d#cd k',k s"xs l(.l f$vf ;)/; j&mj j_nj   24

9   f%% j&& f$$ j__ d## k'' s"" l((;)) f$$ j__ f%% k'' s"" l((36

WORD PATTERNS

10   hap haply happy haptic happen hapless happened happenchance   12

11   lam lamb lame lamp lama lamest lamprey laminated lamentably   24

12   ly sly apply likely lately firmly finely shrewdly helpfully   36

NUMBERS AND SYMBOLS

13   65&5 74&7 20&2 38&3 65&5 74&4 20&2 92&2 83&3 65&5 74&4 29&2   12

14   #7887 #4334 #6776 #5445 #7667 #4554 #8778 #3343 #9889 #2332   24

15   2929 3838 4747 5656 2929 3838 4747 5656 2929 3838 4747 5656   36

WORDS AND PHRASES

16   are in the when they is less else the a be they may to have   12

17   order label invoice shipped operation department perforated   24

18   in just an on the is then and the have it to and for in the   36

SYMBOLS: PAIR PATTERNS

19   ——— *** —*— —*— *See below.   *See insert.   *Turn to page 3.   12

20   ;;; ::: ;:; ;:; Remember to leave two spaces after a colon.   24

21   ——— *** —*— —*— —1— —2— —3— —4— —5— —6— —8— —9— —9— —8— ———   36

SYMBOL SENTENCES

22   Check so that order #3624 is for 9%; order #1544 is for 7%.   12

23   Increase the interest from 7¼% to 8½% by reinvesting today.   24

24   Your 30—payment life insurance policy #55463 is redeemable.   36

  |₁ |₂ |₃ |₄ |₅ |₆ |₇ |₈ |₉ |₁₀ |₁₁ |₁₂

2-A WARMUP   Line—60 • Spacing—1 • Each Line 3 Times

WORDS

1	asdf jkl; asdf jkl; asdf jkl; asdf jkl; asdf jkl; asdf jkl;	12
2	mud kid joy had fix dew big dab ore red raw use rum pry our	24
3	The big red hat did not fit as well in the box on the desk.	36

2-B INVENTORY   Tab—5 • Spacing—2 • Minutes—3 or 5

4   Higher speed in typing results from good stroking; sustained good   **14**
stroking can come only from good posture. Follow the points your   **27**
instructor has given you. Your feet are flat on the floor. You are sitting   **43**
tall, well back in the chair with your shoulders leaning slightly forward.   **58**
Adjust your chair to suit yourself, as your predecessor may have been of   **73**
a different height. The correct position must always be stressed. If you   **88**
are seated in the correct position, your mind will be free to apply itself   **103**
to the work to be done. Be relaxed, but do not slump in the seat.   **116**

5   A high degree of speed as well as the ability to continue typing   **14 130**
correctly for varying lengths of time is your aim. Good posture will help   **29 145**
you not only to improve your skill but also to maintain the pace you   **43 159**
have set for yourself. Good posture at the keyboard is as much a part of   **58 174**
learning how to type with speed and accuracy as is a thorough knowl-   **71 187**
edge of the keys, the correct carriage return, and quick staccato stroking   **86 202**
of the keys. A typist and a machine work together as a unit. Keep your   **101 217**
machine in good condition and yourself in a good posture, and the two   **115 231**
will combine to give you best results.   **122 238**

|1 |2 |3 |4 |5 |6 |7 |8 |9 |10 |11 |12 |13 |14   5.51/1.35

2-C SELECT PRACTICE GOAL   Base It on 2-B Writing

3 MINUTES	If your 3-minute speed is	20–29		30–39		40–49		50–59		60–69		70–up	
	And your error score is	to 6	7 up	to 5	6 up	to 4	5 up	to 3	4 up	to 2	3 up	1	2 up
	Your practice goal should be for	Sp	Ac	Sp	Ac	Sp	Ac	Sp	Ac	Sp	Ac	Sp	Ac

5 MINUTES	If your 5-minute speed is	20–29		30–39		40–49		50–59		60–69		70–up	
	And your error score is	to 7	8 up	to 6	7 up	to 5	6 up	to 4	5 up	to 3	4 up	to 2	3 up
	Your practice goal should be for	Sp	Ac	Sp	Ac	Sp	Ac	Sp	Ac	Sp	Ac	Sp	Ac

27-A   WARMUP
Line—60 • Spacing—1 • Each Line 3 Times

WORDS

1   If you cannot sustain the express, I shall have to halt it.   12

2   Subtract 1 from 9, 6 from 8, 7 from 12, 2 from 7, 3 from 6.   24

3   15 26 35 54 37 15" 26" 35" 54" 37" plus 15' 26' 35' 54' 37'   36

27-B   INVENTORY
Tab—5 • Spacing—2 • Minutes—3 or 5

4   Sometimes when typing very rapidly on a manual typewriter the   13
typist does not strike each key with the same force. In that case a letter   29
may not print or else appear only faintly. It becomes necessary to locate   44
and depress the backspace key with the little finger. It is much easier and   59
faster to do this without looking at the backspace key, though this may be   74
hard to believe at first. Removing your eyes from the copy to locate the   89
backspace key will only cause you to lose time and to break your train of   104
thought, which, of course, can be detrimental to typists.   115

5   The backspacer and the tabulator are timesavers. To save time, how-   15   130
ever, they must be operated by touch. Careful use of the backspacer can   29   144
improve the appearance of your finished work and thus increase your   43   158
value as an expert, rapid, and careful typist.   52   167

6   It is fun to use the margin release so that your line will be finished   15   182
and neat, to use the tabulator to keep lists in order, and to use the back-   30   197
spacer to bring the machine back just in case it has skipped a space or   45   212
two. It is a challenge to learn to be a skilled operator who does not need   60   227
to look away from the copy to operate these speed devices, though it   74   241
might seem easier to use some other system at this time. You will become   88   255
a much better typist when you can strike these keys without looking at   103   270
the machine.   106   273

| 1 | 2 | 3 | 4 | 5 | 6 | 7 | 8 | 9 | 10 | 11 | 12 | 13 | 14 |

5.48/1.40

27-C   SELECT PRACTICE GOAL
Base It on 27-B Writing

3 MINUTES	If your 3-minute speed is	20–29		30–39		40–49		50–59		60–69		70–up	
	And your error score is	to 6	7 up	to 5	6 up	to 4	5 up	to 3	4 up	to 2	3 up	1	2 up
	Your practice goal should be for	Sp	Ac	Sp	Ac	Sp	Ac	Sp	Ac	Sp	Ac	Sp	Ac

5 MINUTES	If your 5-minute speed is	20–29		30–39		40–49		50–59		60–69		70–up	
	And your error score is	to 7	8 up	to 6	7 up	to 5	6 up	to 4	5 up	to 3	4 up	to 2	3 up
	Your practice goal should be for	Sp	Ac	Sp	Ac	Sp	Ac	Sp	Ac	Sp	Ac	Sp	Ac

2-D SPEED BUILDERS

Line—60 • Spacing—1

EASY WORD RHYTHMS

WORDS

6	fad gyp hew icy jar key law mat nip oar pan quo rip six tab	12
7	ache balm clap drop echo fair golf haul idle jamb knit lain	24
8	tudor virus widow angle bogle cubic divot endow flair laugh	36

WORD PATTERNS

9	sor sorriness sorcerer sorghum sorrily sordid sorely sortie	12
10	son comparison jettison treason crimson season prison bison	24
11	sus susceptive suspender suspicion suspense sustain suspend	36

STROKING

12	My thoughts went round and round as we read it and read it.	12
13	They ran back and forth and back and forth most of the day.	24
14	We talked and talked and talked until I could talk no more.	36

PHRASING

15	may fight may throw may ache may bomb may come may flee may	12
16	may laugh may visit may beat may burn may dial may grin may	24
17	may drive may shape may bite may clip may dive may grow may	36

SPEED SENTENCES

18	The two dears paid for their hats when they had some coins.	12
19	One of our tasks is to pay now for a long stay at the lake.	24
20	We must do what we can to see that our pay is not too late..	36

SPACE BAR

21	amends sights laity world rogue cocoa able blot lot dim get	12
22	base clue debt pear next mock word wham task floe deck glad	24
23	dub nap mid was own yes fat awl boo end let net top rag win	36

|1 |2 |3 |4 |5 |6 |7 |8 |9 |10 |11 |12

26-E ACCURACY BUILDERS

Line—60 • Spacing—1

KEYBOARD REVIEW

WORDS

25 The jacket in question had thirty woven, hazel—soft strips. 12
26 f%f j_j f$f j&j d#d k'k s"s l(l ;); f%f j_j f$f j&j d#d s"s 24
27 Quincy enjoyed the five big boxes packed with prize lemons. 36

WORD PATTERNS

28 gad gadolinium gadabout gadwall gadgets gadfly gadder gaded 12
29 hum humanitarian humanistic humdrum humidity humming humble 24
30 rad radioactivity radiation radiance radicle radiate radius 36

NUMBERS AND SYMBOLS

31 #2037 #3861 #7865 #8343 #6127 #9093 #8001 #7127 #9023 #5476 12
32 (3,926) (4,722) (5,277) (6,309) (9,007) (3,681) (7,624) (8) 24
33 $91.13 $83.63 $73.10 $52.42 $92.64 $82.57 $62.41 $30.12 $15 36

WORDS AND PHRASES

34 movements responses ordering dictation dispatch about heads 12
35 all the the head say to a few to and of the and type of the 24
36 function receives similar stimuli clearer brains nerve each 36

CONCENTRATION: EACH LINE NEEDS SIX CAPITALS

37 they rode the "sunshine special" from chicago to st. louis. 12
38 they saw mr. and mrs. wilhelm at the airport in des moines. 24
39 please tell mr. hill that mrs. smith will see him in akron. 36

SYMBOL SENTENCES

40 "Hello," Mary said, "may I speak with Mr. Jackson, please." 12
41 The train should arrive at 8:16, not at 9:16 as I was told. 24
42 Increase the interest from $7\frac{1}{4}\%$ to $8\frac{1}{4}\%$ by reinvesting today. 36

|1 |2 |3 |4 |5 |6 |7 |8 |9 |10 |11 |12

2-E   ACCURACY BUILDERS   Line—60 • Spacing—1

ALPHABET-REVIEW RHYTHMS   WORDS

24	czar drum flax gray iota long mask path quit wave join burn	12
25	fuzz deny garb hark lack quip mast jowl howl oven hoax harp	24
26	leaf lynx oval mown prey silo toga quiz jerk bath clod vine	36

CAPITALS

27	Pat Ray Sal Tab Ula Van Wyn Ace Bee Del Ela Fay Guy Iza Kay	12
28	Mack Mada Omar Page Read Star Toby Ursa Vern Wyna Zack Alma	24
29	Karen Larry Marta Niles Olita Pedro Regan Scott Tessa Ubert	36

ALPHABET-REVIEW SENTENCES: D THROUGH F

30	Deprived daffodils and dandelions were dampened by the dew.	12
31	Every evening eleven enormous elephants escaped extinction.	24
32	Five fox were found fleeing from the forest fire on Friday.	36

PHRASES AND WORDS

33	there are as many as there are number of it may be with the	12
34	table hints extend between columns compact varying possibly	24
35	of course with this plan are easy to in a letter should not	36

CONCENTRATION

36	dais damp dark data date daze ears earn east ease easy each	12
37	face fade fair fake fall fare gait gale gall gang garb gate	24
38	hair hall hail halt hang hard judo jump junk jury just jute	36

REINFORCEMENT

39	The basketball team is expected to do better this year than	12
40	the team did last year. If we recruit more players, we may	24
41	even be able to take the conference and go to the playoffs.	36

|1 |2 |3 |4 |5 |6 |7 |8 |9 |10 |11 |12

26-D   SPEED BUILDERS   Line—60 • Spacing—1

SYMBOL FLUENCY: BASIC REACHES   WORDS

7   f%f j_j f$f j&j d#d k'k s"s l(l f%f ;); f$f j_j d#d j&j s"s   12
8   f4$f j7&j f5%f j6_j d3#d k8'k s2"s l9(l ;0); f4$f j7&j f5%f   24
9   ft5%bf jy6_nj fr4$vf ju7&mj de3#cd ki8',k sw2"xs lo9(.l ;p0   36

WORD PATTERNS

10   ear earn earth earache earmark earmuffs earphone earthquake   12
11   sta stair stale stall stallion stamina stammers standardize   24
12   bou bound bounce bought boulder bouquet boulevard bountiful   36

NUMBERS AND SYMBOLS

13   (292) (383) (474) (565) (161) (232) (383) (484) (575) (292)   12
14   "322" "899" "433" "788" "544" "677" "455" "766" "344" "877"   24
15   -020- -929- -838- -656- -747- -545- -656- -838- -929- -747-   36

PHRASES AND WORDS

16   you must is a to it able to find it have to by touch to the   12
17   body path motion posture fingers position involved handicap   24
18   it is is not is a am with in the the same so that should be   36

SYMBOLS: PAIR PATTERNS

19   $\frac{1}{2}\frac{1}{2}\frac{1}{2}$ (5$\frac{1}{4}$) (3$\frac{1}{4}$) (2$\frac{1}{4}$) (9$\frac{1}{2}$) (8$\frac{1}{4}$) (7$\frac{1}{2}$) (6$\frac{1}{2}$) $\frac{1}{2}\frac{1}{4}\frac{1}{2}$ $\frac{1}{2}\frac{1}{4}\frac{1}{2}$ $\frac{1}{4}\frac{1}{4}\frac{1}{4}$ $\frac{1}{4}\frac{1}{4}\frac{1}{4}$ (4$\frac{1}{4}$)   12
20   3 3/31 6 7/8 7 7/8 4 5/8 3 1/8 6 2/16 5 3/8 /?/ /?/ ??? lll   24
21   Why? Where? Who? What? Why? When? Where? Who? What?   36

SYMBOL SENTENCES

22   My sister-in-law was Mary <u>Dowe</u>, not Mary <u>Dole</u>, please note.   12
23   They selected a new "president" (leader) for every meeting.   24
24   He planned on the 5:16 bus but took the 6:15 train instead.   36
     |₁ |₂ |₃ |₄ |₅ |₆ |₇ |₈ |₉ |₁₀ |₁₁ |₁₂

SKILL DRIVE 3

3-A   WARMUP   Line—60 • Spacing—1 • Each Line 3 Times

WORDS

1   aa ;; ss ll dd kk ff jj gg hh ff jj dd kk ss ll aa ;; ss ll   12

2   cud dog eye flu gas hay ink job key lay mix nod one peg ram   24

3   A rigid penalty may be paid by those who have big problems.   36

3-B   INVENTORY   Tab—5 • Spacing—2 • Minutes—3 or 5

4   Few people ever succeed in business without the trait of courtesy.   15
It will open many doors for you. Your courtesy should ring true to people   30
of all ranks. Give any orders you have to give in the way you like to   44
have them given to you. You will find that people are more willing to   58
work hard at a task when you ask them politely to do it, perhaps as a   72
favor. You must not try to use force in putting over your ideas.   85

5   Courtesy is of first importance at the reception desk and on the   14   99
phone. In fact, you should never fail to be courteous in any situation in   29   114
which you are representing your firm. Courtesy is contagious; therefore,   44   129
if you are courteous to others, they in turn will be courteous to you. It   59   144
will give you control of any problem that may arise.   70   155

6   If you know the names of clients and callers, if you know when   14   169
to knock at closed office doors, if you are pleasant to all with whom you   28   183
come in contact, you will be an asset to the firm that employs you.   42   197
Courteous people avoid noises that disturb others, sharp reprimands, and   57   212
curt answers. You may never be given a responsible position in a firm if   72   227
you lack courtesy. Good manners have a place in the office as well as in   86   241
the home. Courtesy means good manners; it is the stamp of good breeding.   101   256

7   It is important that you exercise this trait when you are talking to 15   271
customers on the phone. In this situation, your voice represents your   29   285
company to the person on the other end of the line. Your manner of   43   299
speaking and the tone of your voice should reflect courtesy.   55   311

| 1 | 2 | 3 | 4 | 5 | 6 | 7 | 8 | 9 | 10 | 11 | 12 | 13 | 14 |

5.42/1.37

3-C   SELECT PRACTICE GOAL   Base It on 3-B Writing

3 MINUTES	If your 3-minute speed is	20–29		30–39		40–49		50–59		60–69		70–up	
	And your error score is	to 6	7 up	to 5	6 up	to 4	5 up	to 3	4 up	to 2	3 up	1	2 up
	Your practice goal should be for	Sp	Ac	Sp	Ac	Sp	Ac	Sp	Ac	Sp	Ac	Sp	Ac

5 MINUTES	If your 5-minute speed is	20–29		30–39		40–49		50–59		60–69		70–up	
	And your error score is	to 7	8 up	to 6	7 up	to 5	6 up	to 4	5 up	to 3	4 up	to 2	3 up
	Your practice goal should be for	Sp	Ac	Sp	Ac	Sp	Ac	Sp	Ac	Sp	Ac	Sp	Ac

26-A   WARMUP   Line—60 • Spacing—1 • Each Line 3 Times

		WORDS
1	My neighbor borrowed my humidor and put it in the corridor.	12
2	Add 7 and 4, 3 and 6, 9 and 10, 5 and 13, 2 and 8, 5 and 1.	24
3	15 26 35 54 37 $15 $35 $54 $37 $54 $37 plus (15) (26) (35).	36

26-B   INVENTORY   Tab—5 • Spacing—2 • Minutes—3 or 5

4   Do not neglect details in your job, even if it becomes necessary to   15
handle them over and over again in the course of a month or a week or   29
even a day. They should receive the same attention that you give to a   43
major task. Routine tasks should receive your best attention.   56

5   Do not go ahead with a piece of work until you understand what is   14   70
to be done and how to do it. This rule will save you much time and   28   84
energy. If you do not grasp what you are expected to do, ask questions   42   98
and clear up your doubts before you begin the work. Many typing errors   57   113
result from the failure to do this. Keep aware of what your work is about   72   128
and the reasons why it should be carried out in a certain way.   84   140

6   Reports that contain figures should be given the closest attention,   15   155
because numerical errors are difficult to detect and can be very serious.   30   170
Correct reports depend on your good attention. For example, if you are   44   184
typing a report of the firm's accounts and you type item #4 as $9.50,   58   198
when it should be $5.90, this error may be overlooked. The report will   72   212
be incorrect even though the totals may be typewritten correctly. The   87   227
typist must be as accurate as the accountant, who sometimes has to spend   101   241
an hour or more locating a 12¢ error. Pay close attention when typing   115   255
figures and avoid errors.   120   260

| 1 | 2 | 3 | 4 | 5 | 6 | 7 | 8 | 9 | 10 | 11 | 12 | 13 | 14 | 5.44/1.41

26-C   SELECT PRACTICE GOAL   Base It on 26-B Writing

3 MINUTES	If your 3-minute speed is	20–29		30–39		40–49		50–59		60–69		70–up	
	And your error score is	to 6	7 up	to 5	6 up	to 4	5 up	to 3	4 up	to 2	3 up	1	2 up
	Your practice goal should be for	Sp	Ac	Sp	Ac	Sp	Ac	Sp	Ac	Sp	Ac	Sp	Ac

5 MINUTES	If your 5-minute speed is	20–29		30–39		40–49		50–59		60–69		70–up	
	And your error score is	to 7	8 up	to 6	7 up	to 5	6 up	to 4	5 up	to 3	4 up	to 2	3 up
	Your practice goal should be for	Sp	Ac	Sp	Ac	Sp	Ac	Sp	Ac	Sp	Ac	Sp	Ac

3-D   SPEED BUILDERS

Line—60 • Spacing—1

EASY WORD RHYTHMS   WORDS

8 pay quo roe sue tie urn vie wit yak zoa aid big cue doe elf   12
9 zinc abut balk chat duck envy find gone hair isle jamb kick   24
10 tutor viand whale audit bight civic dogma ensue fight Japan   36

WORD PATTERNS

11 ive persuasive impressive sensitive thrive revive give hive   12
12 air airsickness aircraft airplane airstrip airtight airflow   24
13 fou foundling fountain fourteen foulard fouling fourth four   36

STROKING

14 We looked on the desk, on the shelf, and even on the floor.   12
15 They may come and go, come and go, and come and go all day.   24
16 We read books, we read papers, and we read magazines today.   36

PHRASING

17 to focus to laugh to shake to throw to beat to dump to hang   12
18 to audit to field to angle to panel to chop to fall to iron   24
19 to shame to shape to sight to visit to daze to grab to joke   36

SPEED SENTENCES

20 The person in the car lent aid to the person who was found.   12
21 They might pay for the work when they go to town for a day.   24
22 Such a sign keeps the right height of the slopes very firm.   36

SPACE BAR

23 pencil finish typing theme major ever mind many now may and   12
24 have take with thus made also line your free neat pear make   24
25 hip any gun nut rid wet pea rob toe ark led fur era cow bet   36

|1 |2 |3 |4 |5 |6 |7 |8 |9 |10 |11 |12

25-E   ACCURACY BUILDERS   Line—60 • Spacing—1

KEYBOARD REVIEW   WORDS

25   Winning the prize entitled me to the six free skiing trips.   12
26   (isn't) —56— (46) 35 & 76 89% $35.33 22# "780" 5 @ 4¢ 3 5/8   24
27   My short report of that big Knoxville game was outstanding.   36

WORD PATTERNS

28   sor sorrow sorority sorghums sorcerer sorrowful sorrowfully   12
29   app appreciation application appliance apperception apparel   24
30   pol policyholder policewoman polygraph polytechnic polarize   36

NUMBERS AND SYMBOLS

31   $90.24 $68.34 $24.96 $80.33 $20.45 $26.88 $38.08 $50.47 $10   12
32   (6,000) (7,000) (8,000) (9,000) (5,000) (4,000) (3,000) (2)   24
33   8,293# 9,304# 6,571# 6,571# 7,482# 1,063# 6,575# 9,302# 46#   36

WORDS AND PHRASES

34   releasing naturally capital finger happen press shift fault   12
35   too high on the fact is from the not kept down this can not   24
36   different alphabet control likely locate looked rapid waste   36

CONCENTRATION: SPELL WORDS FULLY AND CORRECTLY

37   It si thier fond hoep that teh delivrey mya arirve ni time.   12
38   Deer Jawn: Wee shal bee veri plezed too see yu next munth.   24
39   Eye shall W8 4 U; please, this 1 day, do not B L8.   36

SYMBOL SENTENCES

40   We shall need about 110 of "Model 3367" or of "Model 2276."   12
41   I said, "I need only 12 or 13"; and he had 45 on the shelf.   24
42   He was due at 8:08 but arrived "late"--one minute--at 8:09.   36

        |₁ |₂ |₃ |₄ |₅ |₆ |₇ |₈ |₉ |₁₀ |₁₁ |₁₂

3-E   ACCURACY BUILDERS   Line—60 • Spacing—1

ALPHABET-REVIEW RHYTHMS   WORDS

26	aught queue proxy kayak sized rifle mango weave cubic jabot	12
27	dozes bogus lakes corps throw toque toxic veins jelly famed	24
28	augur neigh prism visor wield sixty quick zebra affix judge	36

CAPITALS

29	Lee Martin Nettie Oliver Pamela Robert Sandra Thomas Ursala	12
30	Ari Brenda Calvin Dorene Edward Frieda George Helene Irvine	24
31	Joy Kermit Hector Marvin Natale Oswald Phoebe Ronald Sharon	36

ALPHABET-REVIEW SENTENCES: G THROUGH I

32	Gray ganders gained ground on growing great goose feathers.	12
33	Her husband had heartaches while he handled health hazards.	24
34	Idle ibex intuitively inhabited isolated inclines in India.	36

PHRASES AND WORDS

35	have you ever you may be able will be made you should write	12
36	many free style delete shorter between initially dictionary	24
37	as you want it to with any you should also if you have many	36

CONCENTRATION

38	bale dale gale hale kale pale bold cold fold gold hold mold	12
39	bare care dare fare hare mare bout gout lout pout rout tout	24
40	came dame fame game hame lame bide hide ride side tide wide	36

REINFORCEMENT

41	Our salespeople are very dependable, and are very efficient	12
42	at their work. They have received extensive training for a	24
43	number of various jobs and have attended many meetings too.	36

|1 |2 |3 |4 |5 |6 |7 |8 |9 |10 |11 |12

25-D SPEED BUILDERS

Line—60 • Spacing—1

SYMBOL FLUENCY: BASIC REACHES

WORDS

7   `ft5%f jy6_j fr4$f ju7&j de3#d ki8'k sw2"s lo9(l fr4$f ;p0);`   12

8   `f5%f j6_j f4$f j7&j d3#d k8'k s2"s 19(l f5%f ;0); f4$f j6_j`   24

9   `f%f j_j f$f j&j d#d k'k s"s l(l f%f ;); f$f j_j d#d j&j s"s`   36

WORD PATTERNS

10   `ain maintain curtain obtain retain regain brain train grain`   12

11   `hal hallway halfway halibut halves halo hall hale half halt`   24

12   `sol solo sold solar solve solder solicit solitude solemnize`   36

NUMBERS AND SYMBOLS

13   `$92.23 $73.73 $63.10 $42.42 $82.62 $72.47 $52.31 $20.12 $15`   12

14   `(2,691) (3,832) (6,625) (4,692) (2,472) (6,209) (9,007) (9)`   24

15   `#2739 #4861 #9015 #8083 #9002 #6127 #4383 #2027 #8867 #7377`   36

PHRASES AND WORDS

16   `to cover it for any length that is to keep easy ways are no`   12

17   `ratio remain happens between customers overlooked suggested`   24

18   `keep down to should be be made his should and to are just a`   36

SYMBOLS: PAIR PATTERNS

19   `45¢ 75¢ 85¢ 95¢ 75¢ 35¢ 15¢ 25¢ 65¢ 45¢ 75¢ 85¢ 95¢ 75¢ 35¢`   12

20   `;;; ;¢; ;¢; ;@; ;@; 23 @ 14¢ and 16 @ 17¢ and 10 @ 23¢ ;¢@;`   24

21   `j¢j j¢j j¢j j&j j&j Send 7s 14 @ 28¢ or 29 @ 49¢ right now.`   36

SYMBOL SENTENCES

22   `They thought $55 was too much to "hand out" for a $50 cost.`   12

23   `I lost stock certificate #289 and didn't get a 3% dividend.`   24

24   `Aida (our president)* said, "Let's take a vote on him now."`   36

`|₁  |₂  |₃  |₄  |₅  |₆  |₇  |₈  |₉  |₁₀  |₁₁  |₁₂`

PROGRESS TEST 1

To measure the effectiveness of your practice in
Skill Drives 1, 2, and 3 take two 5-minute
timed writings and average your speed and error scores.

Line—60 • Tab—5 • Spacing—2

WORDS

1   When you develop the proper interest in your company, you 13
will soon be able to devise ways of improving your job and increas- 26
ing your own value. Do not rush too hastily into new methods before 40
your ideas are well thought out or approved by proper authority. When 54
you feel sure that you have a sound idea and that the time has come to 68
present it, take it to the right person. 77

2   It is necessary to know one's job thoroughly in order to recog- 14 91
nize things that can be done or improvements that can be made for 27 104
the company. Initiative without full knowledge sometimes leads to bad 41 118
mistakes. 43 120

3   This trait may be exercised in many ways in the course of a day, 14 134
such as finding work to do if assigned duties are finished, using your 28 148
leisure time for study as a step toward promotion, and doing more than 42 162
you are told to do if there is time. 50 170

4   Take details off your employer's shoulders and relieve him or her 14 184
of routine activities whenever you can. If you prove dependable in 28 198
handling these routine tasks, your employer will soon entrust you with 42 212
more important work. 46 216

5   Interest generates initiative, which leads to advancement, provided 15 231
it is based on sound knowledge. You should learn phases of the business 29 245
other than your own routine tasks so that, in cases of absences, you can 44 260
prove your worth in jobs other than your own. 53 269

6   If you have a new plan that you think will improve the firm's 13 282
business or cut down overhead costs, present it clearly and tactfully 27 296
through proper channels. Some firms have boxes in which employees are 42 311
urged to put their signed suggestions. Often rewards are offered for new 56 325
ideas. 58 327

|1 |2 |3 |4 |5 |6 |7 |8 |9 |10 |11 |12 |13 |14   5.78/1.43

25-A   WARMUP   Line—60 • Spacing—1 • Each Line 3 Times

WORDS

1   We divided the dividend to buy a new boat and a huge divan.   12

2   Adding 25 and 32 and 41 and 52 and 10 gives a total of 160.   24

3   15 26 35 54 37 #15 #26 #35 #54 #37 plus 15% 26% 35% 54% 37%   36

25-B   INVENTORY   Tab—5 • Spacing—2 • Minutes—3 or 5

4   Your health is fundamental to your success. Good health is funda-   14
mental to good work, and you will find it difficult to succeed without it.   29

5   In order to maintain good health, you must get sufficient sleep and   15   44
eat the right foods. Keep in good physical condition so that you can   29   58
arrive at the office in the mornings with vigor, ready for the day. Outdoor   44   73
exercise and sports will keep you in excellent physical shape as well as   59   88
teach you the value of teamwork and fair play. Good health habits in   73   102
your daily living will help you to bear the stress and strain of business   87   116
life. You owe it to yourself and to your employer to keep in good   101   130
physical and mental condition for the position you have undertaken.   115   144

6   Improve yourself both physically and mentally during your leisure   14   158
time. Exercise in the open air as often as you can. Walking at least part   29   173
of the way to and from work is an excellent way to keep fit. Work out a   44   188
budget for your leisure time so that it will afford you the highest returns   59   203
for the time spent. The employee who gets ahead is the one who is able   74   218
to give a full day's work every day.   81   225

|1 |2 |3 |4 |5 |6 |7 |8 |9 |10 |11 |12 |13 |14   5.49/1.39

25-C   SELECT PRACTICE GOAL   Base It on 25-B Writing

3 MINUTES	If your 3-minute speed is	20–29		30–39		40–49		50–59		60–69		70–up	
	And your error score is	to 6	7 up	to 5	6 up	to 4	5 up	to 3	4 up	to 2	3 up	1	2 up
	Your practice goal should be for	Sp	Ac	Sp	Ac	Sp	Ac	Sp	Ac	Sp	Ac	Sp	Ac

5 MINUTES	If your 5-minute speed is	20–29		30–39		40–49		50–59		60–69		70–up	
	And your error score is	to 7	8 up	to 6	7 up	to 5	6 up	to 4	5 up	to 3	4 up	to 2	3 up
	Your practice goal should be for	Sp	Ac	Sp	Ac	Sp	Ac	Sp	Ac	Sp	Ac	Sp	Ac

4-A WARMUP   Line—60 • Spacing—1 • Each Line 3 Times

WORDS

1   waw wbw wcw wdw wew wfw wgw whw wiw wjw wkw wlw wmw wnw wow   12

2   formed print first grade place paper typed using these used   24

3   The cornet is played by many youths in the bands this year.   36

4-B INVENTORY   Tab—5 • Spacing—2 • Minutes—3 or 5

4   When you begin your working career, you may see things that you   14
would like to change. You will not know at the time why things are   27
being done in a certain way, but there will be a reason. Do not be too   42
eager to suggest changes at first. After you have been with a business for   57
some time and you still think you know of a better way to perform a   71
task, then it is fine to suggest a change. You must be tactful in offering   86
suggestions.   89

5   Adaptability is a quality that every employee should have. You will   15   104
be expected to respond readily to changing conditions and to adjust   28   117
quickly to new situations as they arise so that the work may go on   42   131
smoothly. Often you may be called upon to do work that you dislike, or   56   145
you may be asked to follow a new procedure in getting out a report. The   71   160
willingness you show to adapt yourself to these changes may mean a step   85   174
toward promotion. If you balk at new equipment or new ideas, you will   99   188
not be an asset to your company.   106   195

6   The adaptable employee responds quickly and easily to changing   14   209
conditions, to different routines, and to new equipment. You will want to   29   224
cultivate this trait so that you may grow in value to your company and   43   238
thus improve your chances for advancement.   51   246

|1 |2 |3 |4 |5 |6 |7 |8 |9 |10 |11 |12 |13 |14   5.44/1.39

4-C SELECT PRACTICE GOAL   Base It on 4-B Writing

3 MINUTES	If your 3-minute speed is	20–29		30–39		40–49		50–59		60–69		70–up	
	And your error score is	to 6	7 up	to 5	6 up	to 4	5 up	to 3	4 up	to 2	3 up	1	2 up
	Your practice goal should be for	Sp	Ac	Sp	Ac	Sp	Ac	Sp	Ac	Sp	Ac	Sp	Ac

5 MINUTES	If your 5-minute speed is	20–29		30–39		40–49		50–59		60–69		70–up	
	And your error score is	to 7	8 up	to 6	7 up	to 5	6 up	to 4	5 up	to 3	4 up	to 2	3 up
	Your practice goal should be for	Sp	Ac	Sp	Ac	Sp	Ac	Sp	Ac	Sp	Ac	Sp	Ac

PROGRESS TEST 8

To measure the effectiveness of your practice in
Skill Drives 22, 23, and 24 take two 5-minute
timed writings and average your speed and error scores.

Line—60 • Tab—5 • Spacing—2

WORDS

1   As railroads were built across the United States they opened up   14
large farming and ranching areas. They tapped rich forest and mineral   28
resources. They brought better health to the people by hauling a greater   43
variety of foods than had ever been available. Railroads connected the   57
older and more settled parts of the East with the growing regions of the   72
West. Large cities began to grow.   79

2   Today, many forms of transportation compete with railroads as a   14   93
means of public and private transportation; however, the railroads still   28   107
play an important role in the transportation system of the United States   43   122
and most other countries.   48   127

3   There are four forms of railway service available. The first is pas-   15   142
senger service. In the United States, the railroads operate many passenger   30   157
trains daily. Some of these trains run many hundreds of miles, and others   45   172
run for very short distances. There are more than 1,000 station-to-station   60   187
passenger runs of sixty-five miles an hour or faster, and some runs are as   75   202
fast as eighty-two miles an hour from start to stop.   86   213

4   The second type of service available to the public is freight service.   15   228
Out of every dollar the railroads take in, about eighty-five cents is from   30   243
freight. The railroads operate many freight trains each day of the year.   45   258
The third type of service is a special kind of transportation service   59   272
through the Railway Express Agency which the railroads own. This   73   286
agency has offices throughout the United States. The transportation of   87   300
United States mail is the fourth important service performed by the rail-   102   315
roads. Railroads carry a large percentage of the country's mail.   115   328

| 1 | 2 | 3 | 4 | 5 | 6 | 7 | 8 | 9 | 10 | 11 | 12 | 13 | 14 |

6.21/1.52

This page: For speed goal, each LINE 3 times.
For accuracy goal, each GROUP 2 times.

4-D SPEED BUILDERS   Line—60 • Spacing—1

LOCATIONAL SECURITY   WORDS

7   breadth bestow bade bait ball bard bass bad bar bay boy boa   12
8   certain chalet calf clam clip chaf claw car cat cog cot coy   24
9   decline decade damp deer dial diet drab day die din dog dry   36

STROKING: SECOND AND THIRD ROW KEYS

10 They should do their work as well as they did it yesterday.   12
11 People will go if there are good deeds to do for the group.   24
12 Their surprise for the party is at the hall for all to see.   36

WORD PATTERNS

13 pop popularity populace populous popping popgun popper pope   12
14 lea leaning learning leaflet leakage leader learn leak leap   24
15 mil milestone millstone milkweed militia miller millet mill   36

SPACE BAR

16 Ava should. Jim would. Ann said. Jim will. Adela might.   12
17 Stu might. Mavis could. Stu went. Mavis will. Stu shot.   24
18 Irene plays. Tom works. Irene ran. Tom sees. Irene did.   36

ACCELERATION

19 The scenes of the world have been sad in the last few days.   12
20 When the dog barked the fur on the cat's back stood on end.   24
21 They were here and there but never in the same place twice.   36

PHRASES AND WORDS

22 We have all had the in our it might have been in order that   12
23 understand sentences whatever lifetime likewise eight steps   24
24 may be for must be used to that the will be easy should not   36

| 1 | 2 | 3 | 4 | 5 | 6 | 7 | 8 | 9 | 10 | 11 | 12 |

24-E   ACCURACY BUILDERS   Line—60 • Spacing—1

NUMBER FLUENCY   WORDS

26   To 9 or 11 or 13 or 15 or 17 or 19 or 18 or 16 or 14 or 12.   12

27   Go 2 for 1, 6 for 3, 8 for 4, 10 for 5, 14 for 7, 18 for 9.   24

28   1 or 2 or 3 or 4 or 5 or 6 or 7 or 8 or 9 or 10 or 11 or 12   36

WE 23 COMBINATIONS

29   dined 38633 moist 79825 vixen 48236 worry 29446 first 48425   12

30   jumpy 77706 given 58436 pikes 08832 kites 88532 cries 34832   24

31   pumps 07702 honey 69636 burns 57462 linen 98636 seven 23436   36

WORD PATTERNS

32   you youngster yourselves yourself younger youth your you'll   12

33   gen generalization generalize generation generate generator   24

34   lun luncheonette lunchroom lunchtime lunette lunation lunch   36

NUMBERS: PAIR PATTERNS

35   1,112 1,412 1,949 4,471 1,873 1,986 1,959 5,960 5,875 1,776   12

36   2,013 1,637 1,913 6,007 1,401 1,761 1,902 1,843 8,821 1,817   24

37   1,916 9,961 1,952 1,876 7,633 9,651 1,976 5,021 1,965 1,412   36

WORDS AND PHRASES

38   heads about dispatch dictation ordering responses movements   12

39   of the and type and of the a few to say to the head all the   24

40   each nerve brains clearer stimuli function receives similar   36

NUMBER SENTENCES

41   They counted 1 boy and 22 girls, for a total of 23 present.   12

42   The people in the platoon shot 10 rounds each, a 560 total.   24

43   The 44 travelers caught 55 fish, to average 1.25 fish each.   36

   |1 |2 |3 |4 |5 |6 |7 |8 |9 |10 |11 |12

4-E ACCURACY BUILDERS   Line—60 • Spacing—1

ALPHABET-REVIEW: J THROUGH L   WORDS

25	Jumbo jets were justified to join just the jaunts to Japan.	12
26	Kindly Katherine knowingly kidnapped the kaiser's knapsack.	24
27	Little lonely lambs loped lightly on Lealand's lovely land.	36

CONCENTRATION

28	The young secretaries constantly diverted the alert expert.	12
29	Innocence is thought to be an inner, innate feeling by all.	24
30	Warrants are withheld by wardens when they enter the wards.	36

LOCATIONAL SECURITY

31	Bugs were put in boxes as bits of butter were used as bait.	12
32	Cats constantly clawed the customs collector at the circus.	24
33	For the first few months, fat fish and fowl were fed first.	36

WORDS AND PHRASES

34	friend length effort arduous smudges written reason failure	12
35	before it is should not be more if these are longer than it	24
36	doubt decree ignored proofread carefully whatever paragraph	36

CONTINUITY

37	jails jingle jostling juvenile juncture jubilant journalist	12
38	keel kill kind knit knows kidney ketchup kindling kidnapped	24
39	let line lands labored lansing lawsuit lengthens landlocked	36

REINFORCEMENT

40	Some extra salespeople prepared this new invoice form. The	12
41	people were temporary replacements in the office work area.	24
42	The new work area is clearly in need of immediate rezoning.	36

|1 |2 |3 |4 |5 |6 |7 |8 |9 |10 |11 |12

24-D SPEED BUILDERS   Line—60 • Spacing—1

NUMBER FLUENCY: BASIC REACHES   WORDS

8	f5f j6j f4f j7j d3d k8k s2s 1九1 f5f j6j f4f j7j d3d k8k s2s	12
9	j6j f5f j7j f4f k8k d3d 1九1 s2s ;0; j6j f5f j7j f4f k8k d3d	24
10	j77 f44 j66 f55 k88 d33 1九9 s22 ;00 j77 f44 j66 f55 k88 d33	36

WE 23 COMBINATIONS

11	tied 5833 ride 4833 lump 9770 kick 8838 gown 5926 cups 3702	12
12	bins 5862 very 4346 lost 9925 mist 7825 gust 5725 bust 5725	24
13	most 7925 vest 4325 wore 2943 boon 5996 gone 5963 four 4974	36

WORD PATTERNS

14	gar garbage garrison gardener garland garble garage garment	12
15	res respectable resolution respondent respective resiliency	24
16	rad radiance radiation radiator radicle radius radio radial	36

NUMBERS: PAIR PATTERNS

17	3223 8998 4334 7887 5445 6776 4554 7667 4334 8778 2332 9889	12
18	9292 8383 7474 6565 9292 8383 7474 6565 9292 8383 7474 8585	24
19	4747 6565 3838 2929 2020 4747 5656 3838 2929 2020 4747 5656	36

PHRASES AND WORDS

20	of a good all in terms all is what is for hope to is called	12
21	qualities attitude mental value smoothly employee important	24
22	does more can be to have will he and what of it should have	36

NUMBER SENTENCES

23	If we began with 89 and sold 56, we must have 33 left over.	12
24	We had 300, lost 88, found 146, lost 23, found 75; so, 410.	24
25	If we are sure of the 5 and 6 and 0 keys, numbers are easy.	36

|₁ |₂ |₃ |₄ |₅ |₆ |₇ |₈ |₉ |₁₀ |₁₁ |₁₂

5-A   WARMUP   Line—60 • Spacing—1 • Each Line 3 Times

WORDS

1   zaz zbz zcz zdz zez zfz zgz zhz ziz zjz zkz zlz zmz znz zoz   12

2   CUE DAB EAR FAN GNU HAT ICE JAM KID LAG MAD NOT ODD PEP RAN   24

3   At our monthly meeting in town we shall elect our officers.   36

5-B   INVENTORY   Tab—5 • Spacing—2 • Minutes—3 or 5

4   When you are granted an interview, it is a good policy to arrive a   14
few minutes early so that you will be poised and ready for the appoint-   29
ment. You will want to convince your prospective employer that you will   44
be an asset to the firm. Treat the interviewer with respect, but not with   59
fear. Answer all questions to the best of your knowledge, and be prepared   74
to ask a few yourself. No one will expect you to accept a job about which   89
you know nothing.   93

5   Either before or after the interview you will possibly be given an   14   107
application form to fill out. This form should be filled out carefully and   30   123
neatly. Make it a point to print where it asks for printing, to write your   45   138
last name first when so requested, and to write in the proper places on   59   152
the form. Do not leave any of the blanks unfilled. If you cannot give the   74   167
data requested, at least check the blank to show that it has received your   89   182
notice. You may be asked to list a few references on this form. It is best   105   198
not to use the name of anyone for reference unless you have permission   119   212
to do so. Your references should be people in various fields. Do not list   134   227
members of your family as references. The care and neatness you use in   149   242
filling out this form is often taken as a good sign of the kind of work   163   256
you will do on the job.   168   261

|1 |2 |3 |4 |5 |6 |7 |8 |9 |10 |11 |12 |13 |14

5.30/1.31

5-C   SELECT PRACTICE GOAL   Base It on 5-B Writing

3 MINUTES	If your 3-minute speed is	20–29		30–39		40–49		50–59		60–69		70–up	
	And your error score is	to 6	7 up	to 5	6 up	to 4	5 up	to 3	4 up	to 2	3 up	1	2 up
	Your practice goal should be for	Sp	Ac	Sp	Ac	Sp	Ac	Sp	Ac	Sp	Ac	Sp	Ac

5 MINUTES	If your 5-minute speed is	20–29		30–39		40–49		50–59		60–69		70–up	
	And your error score is	to 7	8 up	to 6	7 up	to 5	6 up	to 4	5 up	to 3	4 up	to 2	3 up
	Your practice goal should be for	Sp	Ac	Sp	Ac	Sp	Ac	Sp	Ac	Sp	Ac	Sp	Ac

24-A WARMUP   Line—60 • Spacing—1 • Each Line 3 Times

WORDS

1   aisle blame chair digit elbow forks gowns isles laity neigh   12
2   And 1 and 2 and 3 and 4 and 5 and 6 and 7 and 8 and 9 and 0   24
3   278 271 233 719 902 469 725 588 370 321 514 190 119 718 267   36

24-B INVENTORY   Tab—5 • Spacing—2 • Minutes—3 or 5

4   The history of business education can be separated into three major   15
periods: the early period until about 1850, the business school era from   29
1852 to 1893, and a more recent phase of federal and state aid from 1893   44
to the present.   47

5   During the early period the economy was simple, there was very   14   61
little big business, and there was little industry. The only course in   28   75
business was math, which prepared people to keep an accurate record of   42   89
income and expenses.   47   94

6   The next period began with the opening of one of the schools in   14   108
the Bryant and Stratton chain. This was also the time that typewriters   28   122
first appeared on the market. Business schools flourished during this time.   44   138
The first business-education group was formed, and this group later   57   151
became an avid leader in furthering the growth of the field.   70   164

7   There has been constant and rapid growth in support for programs   14   178
in business since 1893. The first college of business was formed, and   28   192
courses in business were given at the graduate level for those who wished   43   207
to take them.   45   209

|1 |2 |3 |4 |5 |6 |7 |8 |9 |10 |11 |12 |13 |14   5.94/1.46

24-C SELECT PRACTICE GOAL   **Base It on 24-B Writing**

3 MINUTES	If your 3-minute speed is	20–29		30–39		40–49		50–59		60–69		70–up	
	And your error score is	to 6	7 up	to 5	6 up	to 4	5 up	to 3	4 up	to 2	3 up	1	2 up
	Your practice goal should be for	Sp	Ac	Sp	Ac	Sp	Ac	Sp	Ac	Sp	Ac	Sp	Ac

5 MINUTES	If your 5-minute speed is	20–29		30–39		40–49		50–59		60–69		70–up	
	And your error score is	to 7	8 up	to 6	7 up	to 5	6 up	to 4	5 up	to 3	4 up	to 2	3 up
	Your practice goal should be for	Sp	Ac	Sp	Ac	Sp	Ac	Sp	Ac	Sp	Ac	Sp	Ac

5-D   SPEED BUILDERS   Line—60 • Spacing—1

LOCATIONAL SECURITY   WORDS

6   invoice invite ibis idle idol ilex inky icy ilk irk imp ire   12

7   onerous oracle obey oboe oily omit once out oar oak odd oil   24

8   unearth unlike unit upset undo uses uric ulna unbar ugh use   36

STROKING: SECOND AND THIRD ROW KEYS

9   They were so sorry that the jelly had spilled to the floor.   12

10   The judge said that they were fairly tried for their deeds.   24

11   The kite floated swiftly to the opposite side of the field.   36

WORD PATTERNS

12   est shortest longest finest truest nest pest rest vest west   12

13   spo spoiler spoken spook spoof spoor spots spout spoke spot   24

14   ply multiply comply damply simply supply deeply amply apply   36

SPACE BAR

15   The crate of new apples will be sold as soon as it arrives.   12

16   The seller, our boss, is going to New York early next week.   24

17   The book, which is not yet on the market, will soon appear.   36

ACCELERATION

18   They may go to town for the pens if they are not both busy.   12

19   Ella may also work with the form that she got for the firm.   24

20   Olga paid for the eight gowns, but I also paid for the men.   36

PHRASES AND WORDS

21   we have had the to find will be should not be will not that   12

22   ascertain proofread whatever sentence ignored mailed decree   24

23   we had the in a or and be are will not it is not be well an   36

     |₁ |₂ |₃ |₄ |₅ |₆ |₇ |₈ |₉ |₁₀ |₁₁ |₁₂

23-E ACCURACY BUILDERS   Line—60 • Spacing—1

NUMBER FLUENCY   WORDS

26   1 2 3 4 5 6 7 8 9 10 11 12 13 14 15 16 17 18 19 20 21 22 23   12

27   2 4 6 8 10 12 14 16 18 20 22 24 26 28 30 32 34 36 38 40 422   24

28   10 20 30 40 50 60 70 80 90 10 20 30 40 50 60 70 80 90 10 20   36

WE 23 COMBINATIONS

29   mit 785 nib 685 net 635 pet 035 pot 095 rim 487 rot 495 495   12

30   idle 8393 kind 8863 pick 0838 meld 7393 once 9633 risk 4828   24

31   bunk 5768 clew 3932 dole 3993 hope 6903 girl 5849 gist 5825   36

WORD PATTERNS

32   far farfetched farsighted farther farewell farmhand faraway   12

33   jo journalistic journeyman journey journal jogger joviality   24

34   non nonadditive nonbusiness nonaligned nonchalance nonunion   36

NUMBERS: PAIR PATTERNS

35   1,000 3,000 6,000 8,000 1,000 2,000 9,000 4,000 7,000 5,000   12

36   2,039 1,847 6,423 8,347 3,928 4,039 1,756 2,847 3,610 5,756   24

37   9,456 4,586 7,032 2,596 7,834 9,024 6,027 4,908 3,678 2,845   36

WORDS AND PHRASES

38   efficiency increase acquire procure wishes barren knack yet   12

39   is to the first to have along with all for all take hold on   24

40   intelligence competition screening prospect drive much idea   36

NUMBER SENTENCES

41   Jo and Jan live at 124 West 14th Street at Pecan Boulevard.   12

42   Lou lives at 3248 West 8th Street or 5536 East 10th Avenue.   24

43   Sid lives at 1198 South 3rd Street or 189 South 4th Street.   36

      |₁ |₂ |₃ |₄ |₅ |₆ |₇ |₈ |₉ |₁₀ |₁₁ |₁₂

5-E · ACCURACY BUILDERS   Line—60 • Spacing—1

ALPHABET-REVIEW: M THROUGH O   WORDS

24	My many meals are made mostly of meat, mushrooms, and milk.	12
25	None of the ninety nearby neighbors noted the noisy nomads.	24
26	Only once in October ought one occasionally obtain orchids.	36

CONCENTRATION

27	Den fen Hen men Pen ten Yen bat Fat hat Mat oat Pat rat Vat	12
28	Jig rig Wig zig Big dig Fig gig Bam ham Lam jam Ram tan Yam	24
29	Dub hub Nub rub Bub tub Bow how Now row Sow tow Vow wow Cub	36

LOCATIONAL SECURITY

30	The snappy little trapper pulled off the three steel burrs.	12
31	Cutting errors and boosting speed will challenge all of us.	24
32	Three little deer hopped out of the willows into the creek.	36

WORDS AND PHRASES

33	expert writes beauty column frequently asked to judge ideal	12
34	perform person improve achieve exerting developed efficient	24
35	and a good many will still help them to do it at her a more	36

CONTINUITY

36	thought required desired appeals portion public great first	12
37	inexperienced appraisals afternoons practiced Saturday area	24
38	proceedings bookkeeping accountant attending journal orders	36

REINFORCEMENT

39	Any expert who writes a beauty column in magazines or news—	12
40	papers is frequently asked to judge a beauty contest. Most	24
41	of the writers reject such invitations with a firm refusal.	36

| 1 | 2 | 3 | 4 | 5 | 6 | 7 | 8 | 9 | 10 | 11 | 12 |

23-D SPEED BUILDERS

Line—60 • Spacing—1

NUMBER FLUENCY: BASIC REACHES

WORDS

```
8    sw2xs lo9.l de3cd ki8,k fr4vf ju7mj ft5bf jy6nj ;p0/; fr4vf     12
9    s2xs ;0/; d3cd l9.l f4vf k8,k f5bf j7mj j6nj s2xs ;0/; d3cd      24
10   f4vf j7mj d3cd k8,k s2xs l9.l f5bf j6nj ;0/; s2xs l9.l ;0/l      36
```

WE 23 COMBINATIONS

```
11   ken 836 job 795 fit 485 fix 482 gig 585 hot 695 tub 575 575     12
12   sid 283 sox 292 run 476 rug 475 rep 430 sit 285 gut 575 575     24
13   ship 2680 torn 5946 tort 5945 user 7234 void 4983 weir 2384     36
```

WORD PATTERNS

```
14   dir directional directories directive direction direct dire     12
15   jun juncture junction junkyards junior junket jungle junkie     24
16   ja jackhammer jackrabbit jardiniere jasmine jargon jailbird     36
```

NUMBERS: PAIR PATTERNS

```
17   322 899 433 788 544 677 455 766 344 877 233 988 322 899 900     12
18   992 838 747 656 929 838 747 656 929 838 747 656 929 838 747     24
19   202 747 656 383 292 202 474 565 383 292 202 474 565 838 292     36
```

PHRASES AND WORDS

```
20   there will be a for which to put line of that might be made     12
21   put few best product adequate purchase necessary management     24
22   as put out and with the best way what is some need are just     36
```

NUMBER SENTENCES

```
23   Mix l part chemical and 2 parts water for every 1,000 feet.     12
24   They ordered 8 zinnias, 4 roses, 3 tulip bulbs, and l iris.     24
25   With the score 21 to 8, our team has won 9 out of 10 games.     36
```

|1 |2 |3 |4 |5 |6 |7 |8 |9 |10 |11 |12

6-A WARMUP   Line—60 • Spacing—1 • Each Line 3 Times

		WORDS
1	frvf decd swxs aqza jumj ki,k lo.l ;p/; frvf decd swxs aqza	12
2	and bid cut dog elf fig gib ham ivy jam jay key lap men mat	24
3	He wore a jacket and jodhpurs to his job and the jazz show.	36

6-B INVENTORY   Tab—5 • Spacing—2 • Minutes—3 or 5

4   Even the best of typists will make mistakes and will have to use   14
an eraser. Typing success in many positions is measured in terms of   28
quantity and quality of mailable letters. A mailable letter is one that is   43
neatly typed and correct in every respect. It may have a few erasures in   58
it, but they must be done so expertly that it is difficult to find them. If   74
you learn how to make neat erasures you will save yourself the time and   89
effort of retyping many pages. In fact, most employers prefer to have a   103
typist erase rather than to start a new sheet every time he or she makes   118
a mistake.   120

5   There is a knack to making good erasures. You will find it is best   15 135
to leave the letter in the machine until it has been carefully proofread.   30 150
If there is an error, move the carriage or element to one side before you   44 164
begin erasing so that the erasure crumbs will not fall into the typewriter   59 179
and clog the machine. Shields are very useful in making erasures.   73 193
Celluloid shields have cutouts, so that you can isolate letters and figures.   89 209
Select the proper eraser for the type of paper on which you are typing.   103 223
Use a soft eraser on the carbon copy.   111 231

|1 |2 |3 |4 |5 |6 |7 |8 |9 |10 |11 |12 |13 |14   5.42/1.36

6-C SELECT PRACTICE GOAL   Base It on 6-B Writing

3 MINUTES	If your 3-minute speed is	20–29		30–39		40–49		50–59		60–69		70–up	
	And your error score is	to 6	7 up	to 5	6 up	to 4	5 up	to 3	4 up	to 2	3 up	1	2 up
	Your practice goal should be for	Sp	Ac	Sp	Ac	Sp	Ac	Sp	Ac	Sp	Ac	Sp	Ac

5 MINUTES	If your 5-minute speed is	20–29		30–39		40–49		50–59		60–69		70–up	
	And your error score is	to 7	8 up	to 6	7 up	to 5	6 up	to 4	5 up	to 3	4 up	to 2	3 up
	Your practice goal should be for	Sp	Ac	Sp	Ac	Sp	Ac	Sp	Ac	Sp	Ac	Sp	Ac

23-A WARMUP   Line—60 • Spacing—1 • Each Line 3 Times

WORDS

1   kind lark melt naps onyx pare quay rink shun tort undo wilt   12

2   Won 1 won 2 won 3 won 4 won 5 won 6 won 7 won 8 won 9 won 0   24

3   259 268 249 279 126 106 522 628 830 799 566 422 324 881 243   36

23-B INVENTORY   Tab—5 • Spacing—2 • Minutes—3 or 5

4   The way we dress, the food we eat, the work we do, and the views   14
we express all combine to create a style of life. In any given area, it is   29
very probable that the people adhere to the same life-style, but it may   44
also be true that they practice different life-styles. People differ in social   60
background, in modes of dress, in moral codes, and in other life-style   74
traits. A number of life-styles may exist even in the confines of a small   89
town or village. All life-styles have certain traits that identify their   104
existence. The following are some characteristics common to any life-style.   119

5   A life-style maintains certain work ethics or values which may   14   133
dictate that children will not work until they reach a certain age, or it   28   147
may state that women perform certain tasks while men perform others.   42   161

6   Life-styles use communication systems. This trait has been evident   15   176
since people first walked the earth. Societies which did not develop a   29   190
system of writing drew pictures relating to their deeds, actions, and   43   204
beliefs.   45   206

7   A third trait of any life-style is that it has its own pattern of dress.   16   222
People living in tropical climates outfit themselves uniquely for the hot   31   237
climate. Those who reside in the colder regions of the earth maintain   45   251
their own unique modes of dress. This trait is one of the most easily   59   265
identifiable of all life-style characteristics.   68   274

|1 |2 |3 |4 |5 |6 |7 |8 |9 |10 |11 |12 |13 |14   6.01/1.48

23-C SELECT PRACTICE GOAL   Base It on 23-B Writing

3 MINUTES	If your 3-minute speed is	20–29		30–39		40–49		50–59		60–69		70–up	
	And your error score is	to 6	7 up	to 5	6 up	to 4	5 up	to 3	4 up	to 2	3 up	1	2 up
	Your practice goal should be for	Sp	Ac	Sp	Ac	Sp	Ac	Sp	Ac	Sp	Ac	Sp	Ac

5 MINUTES	If your 5-minute speed is	20–29		30–39		40–49		50–59		60–69		70–up	
	And your error score is	to 7	8 up	to 6	7 up	to 5	6 up	to 4	5 up	to 3	4 up	to 2	3 up
	Your practice goal should be for	Sp	Ac	Sp	Ac	Sp	Ac	Sp	Ac	Sp	Ac	Sp	Ac

6-D SPEED BUILDERS

Line—60 • Spacing—1

LOCATIONAL SECURITY

WORDS

6   I could see an angry, blazing fire in the haze of the daze.   12

7   I had opportunity to oppose the opposition of our opponent.   24

8   Your youthful youngsters yearn for those yellow pine trees.   36

STROKING: SECOND AND THIRD ROW KEYS

9   The goal of equal pay for equal work will appeal to us two.   12

10   A trip to the shops took two hours, as we thought it would.   24

11   They told us that he would try to ship the order this week.   36

WORD PATTERNS

12   div diverter division diver divide divine divot divvy dizzy   12

13   ver whatever whomever whenever forever fever lover forgiver   24

14   vic vicarious victimize victorious vicinity victress victor   36

SPACE BAR

15   harm most trap pour ruin news soul lend dark king gain nail   12

16   worry yours sharp paint truth hoist trick kinds stain newly   24

17   poster recall loads steam mixed drain next trip par run new   36

ACCELERATION

18   The five old firms had found the gowns too light for today.   12

19   It is their duty to lend us the right persons for the work.   24

20   I learned how to pass, how to kick, how to run, how to win.   36

PHRASES AND WORDS

21   paper carbon devise stock example received keeping improved   12

22   at any time in the middle just as for the the form and that   24

23   this means other people and how very well to speak know how   36

    |1 |2 |3 |4 |5 |6 |7 |8 |9 |10 |11 |12

22-E   ACCURACY BUILDERS   Line—60 • Spacing—1

NUMBER FLUENCY   WORDS

25	2 4 6 8 10 12 14 16 18 20 22 24 26 28 30 32 34 36 38 40 422	12
26	s2 d3 e3 c3 f4 r4 ab5 g5 t5 h6 n6 j7 u7 m7 k8 i8 19 ;0 p0 q	24
27	3 6 9 12 15 18 21 24 27 30 33 36 39 42 45 48 51 54 57 60 63	36

WE 23 COMBINATIONS

28	cut 375 dye 363 elf 394 end 363 for 494 gob 595 hid 683 683	12
29	mop 790 bud 573 urn 746 hoy 696 nut 675 fox 492 joy 796 796	24
30	pole 0993 room 4997 them 5637 urns 7462 when 2636 wiry 2846	36

WORD PATTERNS

31	que questionnaire questionable question quench queasy query	12
32	ain certain curtain refrain regain retain brain grain train	24
33	ka kangaroos kaolinite kaolin karat kapok kappa kaput karma	36

NUMBERS: PAIR PATTERNS

34	5,242 7,310 8,363 9,113 7,781 8,481 9,264 8,257 6,241 3,012	12
35	9,001 9,093 9,015 2,971 3,861 4,739 7,127 8,343 8,967 2,027	24
36	8,531 7,762 9,481 9,007 2,691 6,832 6,209 7,725 2,472 4,692	36

WORDS AND PHRASES

37	could exist if its managers brainless were as as the survey	12
38	complaints but came with a big up that is point surprises a	24
39	be mutual, in the companies that the managers in the survey	36

NUMBER SENTENCES

40	Totaling 12 and 34 and 56 and 78 and 90 gives 270 as a sum.	12
41	From 100 take 77, add 33, take 44, and add on 55 to get 67.	24
42	Typing a 55 or a 66 may be easier than typing a 56 or a 65.	36

|1 |2 |3 |4 |5 |6 |7 |8 |9 |10 |11 |12

This page: For speed goal, each LINE 2 times.
For accuracy goal, each GROUP 3 times.

6-E   ACCURACY BUILDERS   Line—60 • Spacing—1

ALPHABET-REVIEW: P THROUGH R   WORDS

24 Pat paid appropriate prices for paper to the proper people.   12
25 Queen Quita quickly quipped a quaint quote in a quiet quiz.   24
26 Rural carriers were irregular in preserving their reorders.   36

CONCENTRATION

27 duck dull dump dusk fear feat feed gait gale hale hail hare   12
28 The warden saw the warrant when they entered the warm ward.   24
29 Pay ray Dep hip Nip rip Sip tip Bay day Gay hay Jay may Zip   36

LOCATIONAL SECURITY

30 The shiny earth had relaxed in the rainy days of late fall.   12
31 The hungry caravan dreaded the enemy and evaded the hunter.   24
32 I extended extensive honors for extra theses about honesty.   36

WORDS AND PHRASES

33 cool air into the swept down breath of each night at dusk a   12
34 from the city distant hills at dusk this fresh great firsts   24
35 its pulse and its its heart stir up the city life flowed to   36

CONTINUITY

36 name nabbed noodle national navigator negative nonconductor   12
37 mix mist molar mystery mountaineer motorization modernistic   24
38 oath octapus opener oddities occasion obtrusive observatory   36

REINFORCEMENT

39 Each night at dusk a breath of cool air swept down into the   12
40 city from the distant hills. Each night at dusk this fresh   24
41 life flowed to the city to stir up its heart and its pulse.   36

|1 |2 |3 |4 |5 |6 |7 |8 |9 |10 |11 |12

22-D SPEED BUILDERS   Line—60 • Spacing—1

NUMBER FLUENCY: BASIC REACHES   WORDS

7   sw2s de3d fr4f ft5f jy6j ju7j ki8k lo9l ;p0; sw2s de3d ft5f   12

8   s2s d3d f4f f5f j6j j7j k8k l9l ;0; f4f f5f d3d s2s j6j j7j   24

9   s2s d3d f4f f5f j6j j7j k8k l9l ;0; f4f f5f d3d s2s j6j j7j   36

WE 23 COMBINATIONS

10   we 23 or 94 go 59 do 39 it 85 if 84 so 29 j3 73 u8 78 up 70   12

11   her 634 she 263 vie 483 vex 432 hit 685 nod 693 him 687 687   24

12   find 4863 will 2899 both 5956 most 7925 four 4974 gone 5963   36

WORD PATTERNS

13   wer mower power flower slower answer grower blower follower   12

14   head headed headache headland headlight headdress headfirst   24

15   unk junk bunk chunk flunk plunk spunk trunk shrunk chipmunk   36

NUMBERS: PAIR PATTERN

16   56 47 38 29 56 47 38 29 56 47 38 29 56 47 38 29 56 47 38 29   12

17   67 54 76 45 87 34 97 24 67 54 76 45 87 34 97 24 87 34 97 24   24

18   92 83 65 74 20 29 38 47 92 83 65 74 20 29 38 47 02 38 74 02   36

PHRASES AND WORDS

19   all the parts then send to and a to those of for the as the   12

20   sound staff pain center system senses organization disorder   24

21   of the doing well from its get the as from from our as well   36

NUMBER SENTENCES

22   They bought 4 plums, 6 eggs, 19 cigars, and 16 tulip bulbs.   12

23   Mary got 2 runs and Jack 1 run to win the ball game 8 to 2.   24

24   Adding 39 and 28 and 47 and 56 and 10 gives a total of 180.   36

    |₁ |₂ |₃ |₄ |₅ |₆ |₇ |₈ |₉ |₁₀ |₁₁ |₁₂

To measure the effectiveness of your practice in
Skill Drives 4, 5, and 6 take two 5-minute
timed writings and average your speed and error scores.

Line—60 • Tab—5 • Spacing—2

WORDS

1   Every office has a different procedure for handling mail; but in   14
many cases it will include opening the envelopes, removing the contents,   29
checking for and attaching enclosures, time stamping, and routing.   42
Typists are sometimes called upon to process incoming mail; so learn the   57
correct procedure in your office and follow it carefully. You may also be   72
called upon to handle the outgoing mail. If this is a part of your duties,   87
it is important that you know postal rules and regulations. A copy of the   102
official postal guide will be of great assistance to you in this particular   117
position.   119

2   There is a speedy way to seal envelopes, which you can easily   13   132
master. Spread ten envelopes at a time on a desk so that only the   27   146
gummed flaps are exposed. Then, run a wet sponge over the flaps. With   41   160
one hand, palm down, pick up one envelope at a time; pass it on to the   55   174
other hand with the addressed side against the thumb and the flap down   70   189
against the palm of the hand. You can seal the envelope flap simply by   84   203
closing your hand. Repeat this process until you complete all ten. After   99   218
you moisten a strip of stamps, affix the stamp with one hand and press it   114   233
down with the other, at the same time tearing the stamp loose from the   128   247
strip with the hand in which you hold the strip. You can move the   141   260
envelopes along with your other hand.   149   268

3   In large firms there is a centrally located department that takes care   15   283
of mail handling, but it will be useful to you if you know how this is   29   297
done. In a small business a typist is expected to take care of these   43   311
details.   45   313

4   If you are assigned to a mail desk, take care in opening letters   14   327
written in longhand. They are usually of a personal nature and should be   29   342
given to the employer unopened. You should never open letters marked   44   357
"confidential" unless you have definite permission to do so. Letters   58   371
marked "special delivery" should receive your first attention.   70   383

|₁ |₂ |₃ |₄ |₅ |₆ |₇ |₈ |₉ |₁₀ |₁₁ |₁₂ |₁₃ |₁₄   5.63/1.40

22-A WARMUP
Line—60 • Spacing—1 • Each Line 3 Times

		WORDS
1	belt core dare earn felt gold haze iron join knew lump news	12
2	1 and 2 and 3 and 4 and 5 and 6 and 7 and 8 and 9 and 0 and	24
3	10 21 23 31 32 42 43 44 53 54 65 66 75 76 86 87 95 98 90 97	36

22-B INVENTORY
Tab—5 • Spacing—2 • Minutes—3 or 5

4   Many buildings can provide a great deal more safety if planners 14
take into consideration the proper locations of exits, stairways, areas for 29
storage and handling of dangerous chemicals, and proper arrangement of 43
equipment and fixtures. The type of work, kinds of materials, and number 58
of people involved in each of these areas should also be taken into 72
consideration. Safety precautions can be included in all plans with little 87
or no extra cost in the construction of the building. 98

5   There are times when the importance of the safety of a human life 14 112
is ignored in construction and the emphasis is placed on the effect that 29 127
the equipment or features that provide fire protection may have on the 43 141
beauty and convenience of a building. This is no justification for omitting 58 156
safety features. 61 159

6   A most significant safety feature is the fire alarm system. Fire alarm 15 174
systems of an approved type and design will provide protection of 29 188
extreme value to human life, costly equipment, storage areas containing 43 202
highly flammable materials and dangerous chemicals, and to the building 57 216
itself. The cost of installing and maintaining a system providing suitable 73 232
protection against fire is small when compared with the protection it 87 246
affords. 88 247

| 1 | 2 | 3 | 4 | 5 | 6 | 7 | 8 | 9 | 10 | 11 | 12 | 13 | 14 |

6.30/1.67

22-C SELECT PRACTICE GOAL
Base It on 22-B Writing

3 MINUTES	If your 3-minute speed is	20–29		30–39		40–49		50–59		60–69		70–up	
	And your error score is	to 6	7 up	to 5	6 up	to 4	5 up	to 3	4 up	to 2	3 up	1	2 up
	Your practice goal should be for	Sp	Ac	Sp	Ac	Sp	Ac	Sp	Ac	Sp	Ac	Sp	Ac

5 MINUTES	If your 5-minute speed is	20–29		30–39		40–49		50–59		60–69		70–up	
	And your error score is	to 7	8 up	to 6	7 up	to 5	6 up	to 4	5 up	to 3	4 up	to 2	3 up
	Your practice goal should be for	Sp	Ac	Sp	Ac	Sp	Ac	Sp	Ac	Sp	Ac	Sp	Ac

7-A WARMUP

Line—60 • Spacing—1 • Each Line 3 Times

WORDS

1   aa bb cc dd ee ff gg hh ii jj kk ll mm nn oo pp qq rr ss tt   12

2   abbot tubby occur oddly peels melee offer cuffs foggy muggy   24

3   A haggard aggressor lost luggage and dagger on a foggy day.   36

7-B INVENTORY

Tab—5 • Spacing—2 • Minutes—3 or 5

4   You have observed efficient typists and stenographers at work. They   15
transcribe and type line after line without taking their eyes off the notes   30
or copy. They are using the typewriter completely by touch, not only the   45
letters and numbers of the keyboard but also the tabulator key, the   58
carriage or carrier return lever or key, and the backspace key. They also   73
strike the margin-release key without taking their eyes off the copy.   88

5   If you must remove your eyes from the copy to look for the margin-   14   102
release key, then it is naturally going to take some time to find your   28   116
place again. It is estimated that from ten to twenty-five words, and often   44   132
more, are lost each time you must look at the machine to strike the   58   146
margin-release key. As wasteful as this can be when typing from straight   73   161
copy, you will find it is even more so when you transcribe from short-   87   175
hand notes, for it is really a difficult task sometimes to find your place in   103   191
shorthand notes if you remove your eyes to look for a service key on the   117   205
machine. Keep the carriage or carrier moving steadily. This will be much   132   220
easier when you first learn how to strike the margin-release key by   146   234
touch, and this is easy to do once your mind is made up to do it.   159   247

|₁ |₂ |₃ |₄ |₅ |₆ |₇ |₈ |₉ |₁₀ |₁₁ |₁₂ |₁₃ |₁₄   5.59/1.35

7-C SELECT PRACTICE GOAL

Base It on 7-B Writing

3 MINUTES	If your 3-minute speed is	20–29		30–39		40–49		50–59		60–69		70–up	
	And your error score is	to 6	7 up	to 5	6 up	to 4	5 up	to 3	4 up	to 2	3 up	1	2 up
	Your practice goal should be for	Sp	Ac	Sp	Ac	Sp	Ac	Sp	Ac	Sp	Ac	Sp	Ac

5 MINUTES	If your 5-minute speed is	20–29		30–39		40–49		50–59		60–69		70–up	
	And your error score is	to 7	8 up	to 6	7 up	to 5	6 up	to 4	5 up	to 3	4 up	to 2	3 up
	Your practice goal should be for	Sp	Ac	Sp	Ac	Sp	Ac	Sp	Ac	Sp	Ac	Sp	Ac

PROGRESS TEST 7

To measure the effectiveness of your practice in
Skill Drives 19, 20, and 21 take two 5-minute
timed writings and average your speed and error scores.

Line—60 • Tab—5 • Spacing—2

WORDS

1   Because air travel is the fastest type of transportation, business   14
people and many other persons use it extensively. All major cities are   29
joined by efficient air service. Places that formerly were days apart are   44
now only a few hours away by air. By jet a traveler can fly coast to coast   59
in about five hours. For a long trip, air travel often costs less than some   74
other methods since it does not require expenditures for meals and hotels.   90

2   Air travelers may reserve either coach or first-class seats. Air coach   15   105
fares, sometimes called tourist class, cost less than first-class fares because   31   121
seats are usually smaller (often there are three seats in a row) and fewer   46   136
services are provided. Today many planes, especially jets, have two   60   150
sections—one for coach, the other for first class. Coach travel, therefore,   76   166
is as fast as first class. First-class service on long trips provides superb   91   181
meals and special services; for example, the stewardess will help care for   106   196
infants.   108   198

3   Flight schedules give the time of flights and the stops to be made.   15   213
Passengers wishing a stopover privilege should apply for it when pur-   29   227
chasing tickets. Passengers are required to be at the airport a certain time   44   242
before the departure of the plane.   51   249

4   Persons who travel extensively often use air-travel cards, which   14   263
permit them to charge the costs of flights. If a small airline operates only   30   279
within one state, the air-travel card cannot be used to charge flights.   44   293

5   Many airlines require that returning flights be confirmed at least six   59   308
hours before departure time. To do this, simply call the airline and say   74   323
that you wish to confirm your reservation, which means that you will use   89   338
your ticket.   91   340

|1 |2 |3 |4 |5 |6 |7 |8 |9 |10 |11 |12 |13 |14   6.12/1.44

7-D SPEED BUILDERS   Line—60 • Spacing—1

BALANCED-HAND WORDS   WORDS

6   shake vogue burnt flake tight audit ivory chair digit whale   12
7   quake shame usual worms vivid theme right oaken neigh panel   24
8   elbow gland kendo laity handy flame dogma angle blame chant   36

ALTERNATE-HAND SENTENCES

9   A big neighbor paid for an ancient ornament with six forks.   12
10   I sit and throw rocks by the big lake and handle the ducks.   24
11   The eight chapels sit by the end of the lake and the field.   36

WORD PATTERNS

12   tab tabs taboo tablet tabular tabulate tableware tablecloth   12
13   for form fort forum forced forbid foreign forbear forgiving   24
14   tor actor orator doctor realtor inventor detector detractor   36

LEFT- AND RIGHT-HAND WORDS

15   cast lump acre honk beef poll crew moll card limp daze hull   12
16   bear loom feed loin eggs yolk draw link beds hoop bees hunk   24
17   beat loll face hook ever hymn fast kink cage look deed loop   36

PHRASES AND WORDS

18   sound step strike course fingers without tutored confidence   12
19   same stay bounce reason growth expert position consistently   24
20   body travel just elbows wrist framework correctly important   36

ACCELERATION

21   The signal meant help was on its way to the helpless child.   12
22   My case was adjourned for the day in hopes of new evidence.   24
23   The electors agreed to visit us before the annual election.   36

        |1 |2 |3 |4 |5 |6 |7 |8 |9 |10 |11 |12

21-E ACCURACY BUILDERS

Line—60 • Spacing—1

ALPHABET-REVIEW SENTENCES

WORDS

26 The more proficient a typist becomes, the quicker he or she 12

27 can prepare exact copies of typed work. A typist knows the 24

28 techniques of how to squeeze and spread individual letters. 36

WORD PATTERNS

29 opp oppose opposite oppress opprobrium oppressive opportune 12

30 ess less mess fess guess regress compress progress needless 24

31 ded faded deeded traded bonded loaded evaded hooded blended 36

WORDS AND PHRASES

32 accordingly accordance absolutely apparently adapted advise 12

33 the masons of suspension suspects the the suspicious parson 24

34 pantomimed confused people the panelists in a panic pending 36

KEY CONTROL: INDIVIDUAL LETTERS V, W, AND X

35 V via vial visor virus visit vivid vodka vogie vogue vacant 12

36 W wit wig worm work west with wall work write works world's 24

37 X six mix lax index mixed fixed luxury duplex excess expire 36

CONCENTRATION: INSERT MISSING LETTERS

38 I sh-ll h-v- t- -sk th-m t-d-y f-r - n-w c-py -f y--r b--k. 12

39 Th-y sh--ld s--n b- -ble t- r-p-rt th- r-s-lts -f my t-sts. 24

40 P-ns --- p-p-r w-ll b- k-pt -n th- f-le- b- --- bla-k d-or. 36

SHARP STROKING

41 The suspicious parson suspects the suspension of one mason. 12

42 The panelist pantomimed confused people in a pending panic. 24

43 The hungry caravan dreaded the enemy and evaded the hunter. 36

|₁ |₂ |₃ |₄ |₅ |₆ |₇ |₈ |₉ |₁₀ |₁₁ |₁₂

7-E   ACCURACY BUILDERS

Line—60 • Spacing—1

ALPHABET-REVIEW: S THROUGH U

WORDS

24 Sandy's steady shears silently slit Sylvia's shorn shreads.   12
25 Three little letters told the story--a matter of attitudes.   24
26 Unluckily Uncle upset Ula until unnecessary ulcers erupted.   36

CONCENTRATION

27 The inspector saw a defect and marked the object imperfect.   12
28 The immigrant immediately immersed the washcloths in water.   24
29 Shrink, shrank, shrunk are the principal parts of the verb.   36

ONE-HAND-WORD SENTENCES

30 Gerta saw a bear on a hill, bagged him, and dragged him in.   12
31 In fact, you saw a deer jump in my carts and eat my onions.   24
32 Joy saw a puny pink bear in a water pool up on Carter Hill.   36

CONTINUITY

33 ill ideal inquiry intention insurance immediate interesting   12
34 mad memo market medical maintenance manufacturer multiplier   24
35 canny tension attending conventions distributor conclusions   36

WORDS AND PHRASES

36 learned release margin length beyond class extra there five   12
37 different looking likely struck locate both found view when   24
38 quickest struggle willing because without direct must do so   36

REINFORCEMENT

39 If you ever find that you may visit our campus, I hope that   12
40 you will let me know; I should like to show you some of the   24
41 sights and have you meet the men and women for whom I work.   36

|1 |2 |3 |4 |5 |6 |7 |8 |9 |10 |11 |12

21-D   SPEED BUILDERS

Line—60 • Spacing—1

JUMP WORD SENTENCES

WORDS

8   When they showed us the clay bowls and urns they had found,   12

9   we knew at once that they were the same ones we had left on   24

10   the small island in the lake.   30

BOUNCE-BACKS

11   Jerk Joke Jowl Judo Knot Knit Knee Kick Lace Lame Land Laud   12

12   Maid Main Mane Mash Neat Navy Noon Nose Once Oily Obey Oval   24

13   Pica Peer Peel Pear Pawn Rose Rote Rung Sack Sail Salt Scan   36

WORD PATTERNS

14   res responsible restaurant restraint resume respond restive   12

15   gar gardener garment gardenia gargle garlic garnish garbage   24

16   non nonenforceable nonetheless nonmetallic nonplus nonsense   36

PHRASES AND WORDS

17   discerned the glory the ancient of story the rectory course   12

18   is to in the and the you can so that by what by your at the   24

19   subscribe to we may the new directory at a factory keyboard   36

OVERCOMING JAMMING OF KEYS

20   The boy patient did work for the girl with the cow and yak.   12

21   The bowl of clams burned, and an iguana quenched the flame.   24

22   When it is his turn to work, Rod and I go down to the lake.   36

ADJACENT LETTER SENTENCES

23   He discerned the glory of the ancient story at the rectory.   12

24   I may subscribe to the new factory directory at a discount.   24

25   Each of the girls wishes to work on a new form for the job.   36

| 1 | 2 | 3 | 4 | 5 | 6 | 7 | 8 | 9 | 10 | 11 | 12 |

8-A   WARMUP

Line—60 • Spacing—1 • Each Line 3 Times

WORDS

1   aa ;; qq pp zz // ss ll ww oo xx .. dd kk ee ii cc ,, ff jj   12

2   allow shall jimmy dummy penny annex spool goods upper happy   24

3   My letter was thrown or dropped suddenly by a yellow plane.   36

8-B   INVENTORY

Tab—5 • Spacing—2 • Minutes—3 or 5

4   Your employer expects you to be dependable. This trait will help   14

you to succeed in your job and will win you the respect of your   27

employer and fellow workers. It means you can be depended upon to   40

report for work on time and to stay on the job during the working hours   55

that your employer has set. It also means that you can be depended upon   69

to do the right thing at the right time. Give just as much attention to the   85

small task as you would to a major one. Minor tasks are often more   98

important than you think. You may not realize the importance of keeping   113

a good stock of forms on hand until you need them for a rush job and   127

find there are not enough. Others may have depended upon your taking   141

prompt care of that small task. People who are dependable   153

see every task through to the finish. You must follow directions to the   167

letter and abide by the policies of your firm.   177

5   Prove to your employer that you can be depended on to type mail-   14   191

able letters and accurate reports. Once your employer is convinced that   28   205

you are dependable, he or she will give you more responsible duties. In   43   220

order to succeed in business, you must be dependable in all respects.   57   234

6   A loyal attitude toward the firm for which you work is a prime   14   248

virtue. If you find yourself in a position where you feel you cannot give 29   263

your employer complete loyalty, it is wise to look for another job.   42   276

|1 |2 |3 |4 |5 |6 |7 |8 |9 |10 |11 |12 |13 |14   5.41/1.40

8-C   SELECT PRACTICE GOAL

Base It on 8-B Writing

3 MINUTES	If your 3-minute speed is	20–29		30–39		40–49		50–59		60–69		70–up	
	And your error score is	to 6	7 up	to 5	6 up	to 4	5 up	to 3	4 up	to 2	3 up	1	2 up
	Your practice goal should be for	Sp	Ac	Sp	Ac	Sp	Ac	Sp	Ac	Sp	Ac	Sp	Ac

5 MINUTES	If your 5-minute speed is	20–29		30–39		40–49		50–59		60–69		70–up	
	And your error score is	to 7	8 up	to 6	7 up	to 5	6 up	to 4	5 up	to 3	4 up	to 2	3 up
	Your practice goal should be for	Sp	Ac	Sp	Ac	Sp	Ac	Sp	Ac	Sp	Ac	Sp	Ac

21-A WARMUP

Line—60 • Spacing—1 • Each line 3 Times

WORDS

1 ze ze oze doze haze maze sizes no no not note nose snob snow   12

2 ve ve eve pave live dove gives ny ny any tiny many zany deny   24

3 be be bed bell beam beep beans mp mp imp damp ramp tamp camp   36

21-B INVENTORY

Tab—5 • Spacing—2 • Minutes—3 or 5

4   We all endeavor to produce mailable copy, and we work very hard   14
to proofread our work in the hope that we will be able to find any errors   29
we have made and correct them. No matter how effectively we proofread,   43
however, we may overlook an error.   50

5   Proofreading is a major responsibility of a secretary, for it is this   15   65
individual who usually is the last to glance at copy before it is sent in   30   80
the mails. To assist a typist or secretary in the job of proofreading, the   45   95
following data reveals some of the most frequently undetected typewriting   60   110
errors that are missed in proofreading.   68   118

6   The dateline and address line are commonly overlooked when copy   14   132
is being proofread. We seem to take for granted that this material is correct   30   148
and are concerned only about the body of the letter. What could be more   44   162
serious an error, however, than to misspell an addressee's name?   57   175

7   Omission errors are also quite common. These mistakes can consist   14   189
of something as small as only a missing letter or can be as serious as a   29   204
missing word, phrase, or thought. The secretary must be certain to read   44   219
copy for content to insure that these errors are not overlooked.   56   231

|1 |2 |3 |4 |5 |6 |7 |8 |9 |10 |11 |12 |13 |14   5.75/1.56

21-C SELECT PRACTICE GOAL

Base It on 21-B Writing

3 MINUTES	If your 3-minute speed is	20–29		30–39		40–49		50–59		60–69		70–up	
	And your error score is	to 6	7 up	to 5	6 up	to 4	5 up	to 3	4 up	to 2	3 up	1	2 up
	Your practice goal should be for	Sp	Ac	Sp	Ac	Sp	Ac	Sp	Ac	Sp	Ac	Sp	Ac

5 MINUTES	If your 5-minute speed is	20–29		30–39		40–49		50–59		60–69		70–up	
	And your error score is	to 7	8 up	to 6	7 up	to 5	6 up	to 4	5 up	to 3	4 up	to 2	3 up
	Your practice goal should be for	Sp	Ac	Sp	Ac	Sp	Ac	Sp	Ac	Sp	Ac	Sp	Ac

8-D SPEED BUILDERS   Line—60 • Spacing—1

BALANCED-HAND WORDS   WORDS

7   land kept jamb idle half goal fuel envy disk chap bowl airy   12
8   halt iris jams keys lake mend glen form dock clam busy auto   24
9   rich soap torn urns vial worm yaks maid name odor pale quay   36

ALTERNATE-HAND SENTENCES

10 The lane to the lake may make the auto turn and go to town.   12
11 They go to the lake by bus when they work for Jan or Bobby.   24
12 May Juan and Elda go to the lake if Bob and Joel take them?   36

WORD PATTERNS

13 lly jolly ideally legally specially officially industrially   12
14 aff affix affair afford affirm affects affection affliction   24
15 ert revert divert covert assert alert expert invert convert 36

LEFT- AND RIGHT-HAND WORDS

16 bat mum far hip dead kip base holy adaze July cabaret imply   12
17 cat hop bet lip dear ink deer kill abase join cabbage knoll   24
18 gas you dew kin fade joy deaf lion cadet lily baggage jumpy   36

PHRASES AND WORDS

19 palms barely curved wrists running pausing bicycle position 12
20 loop bounce barely thumbs slashes explode grasping downward   24
21 term speck burned linger release flicking whacking consider   36

ACCELERATION

22 The rug firm is to pay us for the work if the work is good.   12
23 I just won and lost, won and lost, won and lost all season.   24
24 Important persons will receive credit when they ask for it.   36

|1 |2 |3 |4 |5 |6 |7 |8 |9 |10 |11 |12

20-E   ACCURACY BUILDERS   Line—60 • Spacing—1

ALPHABET-REVIEW SENTENCE   WORDS

25 The major feature of the wonderful exhibition was the large   12
26 painting with the azure background; one of my acquaintances   24
27 found it too expensive to buy.   30

WORD PATTERNS

28 eli elite elicit eligible elixir elision elimination elided   12
29 hon hone honk honey honorary honorarium honorable honeymoon   24
30 ext extol extort extent extinct external exterior extension   36

WORDS AND PHRASES

31 difficult initiating envision standard diagonal conclusions   12
32 can be were cut off is the if you try this a few a few were   24
33 aims sharp flash bounce toward helpful necessary accomplish   36

KEY CONTROL: INDIVIDUAL LETTERS S, T, AND U

34 S sir sob six sick such soap socks shake shame social spoke   12
35 T tub tie toe tick torn town tight turns towns theme theory   24
36 U us urn undo usual user usurp union unable uxorial utterly   36

CONCENTRATION: INSERT MISSING LETTERS

37 S-- w-ll n-t t-ll th-m -nl-ss - r-c--v- th- r-p-rt -n t-m-.   12
38 D--r G-org-: Pl--s- l-t u- hav- --r r-p-rt b- r-t-rn m--l.   24
39 Pl--s- sh-w m- t-- w-rk sch-d-l-- -s s--n -s y-- m-k- th-m.   36

SHARP STROKING

40 You and I may go to the game after you have mowed the lawn.   12
41 The owl did laugh when the ox got thrown down by Town Lake.   24
42 Initiating action for their idea was difficult to envision. 36
    |1 |2 |3 |4 |5 |6 |7 |8 |9 |10 |11 |12

8-E   ACCURACY BUILDERS   Line—60 • Spacing—1

ALPHABET-REVIEW: V THROUGH X   WORDS

25   Vivacious voters value vision, verve, and very vivid vigor.   12

26   We want a welcome when we work westward with new waterways.   24

27   The excommunicated xylophonist excerpted the right example.   36

CONCENTRATION

28   me may melt make mangy mantle nays name neigh naught orient   12

29   of owl ogle odor oaken pay pane pale penal panels que quake   24

30   quay quench rid rush rosy right ritual six sex such than to   36

ONE-HAND-WORD SENTENCES

31   The mill rests on the hill against the seas of azure water.   12

32   The loony bat looks at the ink vase carried in my red cart.   24

33   Lily bet on a puny wet pony in water polo at Webster Knoll.   36

CONTINUITY

34   an aye auto airy audit ambush burner bowls bullet bulky bud   12

35   cot city coal chair chapel dismal divot dish duck due eight   24

36   go gig gown glen girls gospel handle handy held hang hay he   36

WORDS AND PHRASES

37   evaluate recognize chances market success buyer costly most   12

38   part of the to be has that in it of a that they were is the   24

39   thoughts required desired portion public appeal first great   36

REINFORCEMENT

40   The teacher went over the project so that the class was not   12

41   confused on the right way to prepare the project. It was a   24

42   long assignment to be done in the home the next four weeks.   36

20-D SPEED BUILDERS   Line—60 • Spacing—1

JUMP WORD SENTENCES   WORDS

7   We shall do all that we can to see that your order is given   12
8   top priority. I am sure that you can count on its arriving   24
9   by the time you will need it.   30

BOUNCE-BACKS

10 Ache Ague Ahoy Alum Base Bass Bath Bear Camp Calm Cash Card   12
11 Data Daze Deaf Deck East Echo Edge Epic Firm Flag Flat Flax   24
12 Gang Gild Glad Glee Hale Hare Harp Haze Iron Isle Item Iota   36

WORD PATTERNS

13 dir dire dirndl direction dirigible directories dirty dirge   12
14 far farsighted farfetched farther farewell farmer farm fare   24
15 th path lath math pith Ruth wrath heath mouth fourth health   36

PHRASES AND WORDS

16 executive secretary nothing through leave motto all nothing   12
17 closing talked peach every speak while asked walk wise door   24
18 hope to find what is on the list for all in terms of in any   36

OVERCOMING JAMMING OF KEYS

19 Their leader held that their eighth right is also to fight.   12
20 Pam Hale slept by the lame dog when it bit their cow's leg.   24
21 A male turkey may fight a snake for a dish of corn and ham.   36

ADJACENT LETTER SENTENCES

22 It did not seem worthwhile to make the trips into the town.   12
23 It is not right to turn down the work when it pays so well.   24
24 It is his duty to do his duty--but not his duty to like it.   36

    |₁ |₂ |₃ |₄ |₅ |₆ |₇ |₈ |₉ |₁₀ |₁₁ |₁₂

9-A   WARMUP

Line—60 • Spacing—1 • Each Line 3 Times

WORDS

1	aa;; ssll ddkk ffjj gghh ffjj ddkk ssll aa;; ssll ddkk ffjj	12
2	error merry guess asset otter patty fuzzy dizzy speed silly	24
3	He is irresponsible, irrational, and irritating to his pal.	36

9-B   INVENTORY

Tab—5 • Spacing—2 • Minutes—3 or 5

4   Because an employer is usually extremely busy, he or she can take   14
time to give directions only once. You should make it a practice to listen   29
attentively and to take careful notes. Do not depend upon your memory.   44
If you are in doubt, do not be afraid to ask questions; but hear the   58
answers so that you will not have to ask the same questions again. Very   72
few people give explicit directions, though they may think that they are   87
being very explicit. Make sure that you get it right the first time. Review   103
your directions before you begin the work.   111

5   Your employer has the right to expect your complete attention on   14   125
the job. He or she expects you to hear and to heed what you are told. An   29   140
ability to take instructions is one of the most valuable assets of an effi- 44   155
cient typist. Good attention is a trait that will aid you in achieving your 59   170
goal.   61   172

6   Attention implies more than merely listening to instructions. It also 15   187
means following them out correctly in detail. It means giving care to the   30   202
assignment and turning out neat, mailable letters and accurate reports.   45   217
Good attention is a trait that should be developed as early as possible. It 60   232
will save you many mistakes and will make your work easier. Good   73   245
results depend on good attention. Every letter or report that you type   88   260
should reflect the good attention that you gave to the task.   100   272

|1 |2 |3 |4 |5 |6 |7 |8 |9 |10 |11 |12 |13 |14   5.71/1.46

9-C   SELECT PRACTICE GOAL

Base It on 9-B Writing

3 MINUTES	If your 3-minute speed is	20–29		30–39		40–49		50–59		60–69		70–up	
	And your error score is	to 6	7 up	to 5	6 up	to 4	5 up	to 3	4 up	to 2	3 up	1	2 up
	Your practice goal should be for	Sp	Ac	Sp	Ac	Sp	Ac	Sp	Ac	Sp	Ac	Sp	Ac

5 MINUTES	If your 5-minute speed is	20–29		30–39		40–49		50–59		60–69		70–up	
	And your error score is	to 7	8 up	to 6	7 up	to 5	6 up	to 4	5 up	to 3	4 up	to 2	3 up
	Your practice goal should be for	Sp	Ac	Sp	Ac	Sp	Ac	Sp	Ac	Sp	Ac	Sp	Ac

20-A WARMUP   Line—60 • Spacing—1 • Each Line 3 Times

WORDS

1   abcdefghijklmnopqrstuvwxyz abcdefghijklmnopqrstuvwxyz abcde   12

2   auto born burn city dish envy form girl held pale pane this   24

3   A kind kindergarten teacher is loved by all his tiny pupils.   36

20-B INVENTORY   Tab—5 • Spacing—2 • Minutes—3 or 5

4   Many motions are used in typewriting—many more than just   13
striking the letter or number keys. Touch typewriting means not looking   27
at the keys when striking them. It is important to remember that all   41
motions at the typewriter are to be made by touch. This relieves your   55
mind of the problem of hunting for each key and saves time.   68

5   The correct carriage return, if made by touch, saves time. Good   14   82
posture relieves tension and helps you relax. This also saves time. Know-   29   97
ing the location of the tabulator key and using it correctly saves a great   44   112
deal of time. The tabulator key is very useful to you in your work. After   59   127
tab stops have been set you do not have to look at the tab key when   73   141
striking it. Use this key by touch, and you will add greatly to your   87   155
speed. The touch system depends upon the correct use of the tabulator   101   169
key and the carriage return key or lever as well as the rapid stroking of   116   184
the keys—all by touch.   121   189

6   You will become a better typist if you do not look at the keys.   14   203
Often in the business world you will be asked to type difficult and   28   217
unfamiliar material quickly. It is then that you will see how truly helpful   43   232
the touch system is. The touch system permits you to give all your   57   246
attention to the copy while your fingers type swiftly and accurately,   71   260
moving over the keys with ease.   77   266

| 1 | 2 | 3 | 4 | 5 | 6 | 7 | 8 | 9 | 10 | 11 | 12 | 13 | 14 |

5.73/1.33

20-C SELECT PRACTICE GOAL   Base It on 20-B Writing

3 MINUTES	If your 3-minute speed is	20–29		30–39		40–49		50–59		60–69		70–up	
	And your error score is	to 6	7 up	to 5	6 up	to 4	5 up	to 3	4 up	to 2	3 up	1	2 up
	Your practice goal should be for	Sp	Ac	Sp	Ac	Sp	Ac	Sp	Ac	Sp	Ac	Sp	Ac

5 MINUTES	If your 5-minute speed is	20–29		30–39		40–49		50–59		60–69		70–up	
	And your error score is	to 7	8 up	to 6	7 up	to 5	6 up	to 4	5 up	to 3	4 up	to 2	3 up
	Your practice goal should be for	Sp	Ac	Sp	Ac	Sp	Ac	Sp	Ac	Sp	Ac	Sp	Ac

9-D SPEED BUILDERS   Line—60 • Spacing—1

BALANCED-HAND WORDS   WORDS

7   idle kept half fuel envy land jamb goal disk chap bowl airy   12
8   glen iris keys mend lake jams halt dock busy auto clam form   24
9   rich torn vial yaks worm urns soap quay maid name odor pale   36

ALTERNATE-HAND SENTENCES

10 The man and the girl rush down the dismal path to the town.   12
11 Jose and the six girls got rid of the sign and the problem.   24
12 He may pay for the bushel of corn when he visits the field.   36

WORD PATTERNS

13 cha chat chasm chair chalk chapel chaser chapters character   12
14 inn inns inner innate innocent innuendo innovates innocence   24
15 war wares warm ward warble warmth warship warfare warehouse   36

LEFT- AND RIGHT-HAND WORDS

16 nippy carts milky dates phony draft mummy cafes nylon brags   12
17 loony gears lumpy gates holly carve union draws jolly cards   24
18 abate hilly facts Ginny lymph cedar holly caves jolly exert   36

PHRASES AND WORDS

19 to achieve is not for it in all his work his boss is always   12
20 dreams extremely sincerity possesses constantly genuineness   24
21 demand service shelves another performed task select detail   36

ACCELERATION

22 The tour is a long one that will let us see the old sights.   12
23 It is a good thing to be able to laugh when one is serious.   24
24 We knew it would rain, and rain it did in that second half.   36

   |1 |2 |3 |4 |5 |6 |7 |8 |9 |10 |11 |12

19-E   ACCURACY BUILDERS   Line—60 • Spacing—1

ALPHABET-REVIEW SENTENCE   WORDS

24	A luxuriant ray of beautiful sunshine, making lazy patterns	12
25	on the country road, brought the sparkle of fine jewelry to	24
26	a million quivering dewdrops.	30

WORD PATTERNS

27	fac face fact facial facile faction factual factory faculty	12
28	lim lima lime limb limber limeade limelight limestone limit	24
29	pho photo phonetic phosphate photocell photostat photoflash	36

WORDS AND PHRASES

30	idea fork prong slant equal sheets bottom distance counting	12
31	if very is the most to your should be of the seems to of it	24
32	exchange important equipped thousand business employee once	36

KEY CONTROL: INDIVIDUAL LETTERS P, Q, AND R

33	P pal pale pane panel plans pang pays papa penalty problems	12
34	Q quay quit quake quite quiet quote quick quarter quarterly	24
35	R rob rod row rug rub rye red risk rose rocks right rituals	36

CONCENTRATION: INSERT MISSING LETTERS

36	It occurred to me ———— the accounting division had success.	12
37	——— tabulation —— tabled ——— other tabulation computations.	24
38	The lane to ——— lake ——— make the auto turn ——— to —— town.	36

SHARP STROKING

39	Six sorority gals wish to do busy chapel and neighbor work.	12
40	The crowd appraised the last appearance and then applauded.	24
41	Whatever you do, deliver my silver whenever he asks for it.	36

|1 |2 |3 |4 |5 |6 |7 |8 |9 |10 |11 |12

9-E ACCURACY BUILDERS   Line—60 • Spacing—1

ALPHABET-REVIEW: Z THROUGH B   WORDS

25 Dazed by the haze, Zeta zigzaged her way to her jazz class.   12
26 Advertise Airlines' aviation agency announces all arrivals.   24
27 Bob became bitter because Beth baked butterscotch brownies.   36

CONCENTRATION

28 Aid ail Aim air Bar bat Bay bag Cab can Car cat Did dig Dim   12
29 Beg bed Bet bit Cot cog Cob din Dip die Fan far Fat gab Gap   24
30 Fir fix Fox gay Gag had Hay Ice jam Lag mad Not odd Cue ran   36

ONE-HAND-WORD SENTENCES

31 Eva saw bees jump in the red vases and wade in oily waters.   12
32 Barbara sees the need to cart the red kiln up to the hills.   24
33 They join to brag of dumping their debts at Eastferd's Inn.   36

CONTINUITY

34 tabulation computation excitement excavation excelled ideal   12
35 shampoo shammy shamble shapable sharpen shatter shaver shay   24
36 streetlight streetcar strengthen strength strenuous stretch   36

WORDS AND PHRASES

37 to get shown price public willing because product expensive   12
38 of firm banks borrow provide company insurance requirements   24
39 speedy business reply card envelope justifiable postage can   36

REINFORCEMENT

40 When you get to the office of the new firm, try to find the   12
41 name of the new manager before you ask for him. If you can   24
42 ask for him by name, you are more likely to get to see him.   36

|1 |2 |3 |4 |5 |6 |7 |8 |9 |10 |11 |12

19-D SPEED BUILDERS

Line—60 • Spacing—1

JUMP WORD SENTENCES

WORDS

6	We ran the risk and put in an hour or so looking around the	12
7	cabin. We took it apart, I tell you; and yet we could find	24
8	no sign of the rug he wanted.	30

BOUNCE-BACKS

9	Ash Awl Bar Bug Big Boo Box Cry Cue Cut Dim Dip Dub Eye Ego	12
10	Flu Fog Fox Get Gym Gun Hoe Hop Hub Ilk Ink Irk Jar Jet Jog	24
11	Key Kid Kit Lad Law Lax Mat Mix Mod Nay Nip Nod Oak Oil Ore	36

WORD PATTERNS

12	kin kindliness kindhearted kinfolk kinkier kindred kingfish	12
13	hin hint hints hinge hinges hinted hinder hinting hindrance	24
14	ght might right sight tight caught bright slight playwright	36

PHRASES AND WORDS

15	efficiency indention pitched example spotted minute teacher	12
16	who get in the do so they have made they are for each is to	24
17	practiced technique perfect motion fourth finger hinge time	36

OVERCOMING JAMMING OF KEYS

18	The rock lane forms a path to the lake for the boy to fish.	12
19	The girl may bid for the maps when she pays the duty woman.	24
20	The idle auto is by the right turn of the island lake lane.	36

ADJACENT LETTER SENTENCES

21	The men will have to go to town and work in the town parks.	12
22	She lost the keys to the boat down at the lake by the dock.	24
23	We do not know, and we must know, what they plan to do now.	36

|1 |2 |3 |4 |5 |6 |7 |8 |9 |10 |11 |12

Lorenza M. Padley

PROGRESS TEST 3

To measure the effectiveness of your practice in
Skill Drives 7, 8, and 9 take two 5-minute
timed writings and average your speed and error scores.

Line—60 • Tab—5 • Spacing—2

WORDS

1	Electric typewriters are rapidly replacing manual typewriters for	14
	business use. Business has found that the electric machine assures neater	29
	work and higher production rates. It also boosts the morale of typists. It	45
	has been found that a typist can make the adjustment to the electric	58
	machine in only a few hours.	64

2	The quality of work produced on the electric is the same whether it	15	79
	is typed by an expert or a less-skilled typist. Typists enjoy the ease of	30	94
	operation that the electric makes possible. Reduced effort and lessened	45	109
	fatigue permit the typist to attain greater speed.	56	120

3	One of the chief features of the electric model is the carriage return	15	135
	key. A flick of the key with the right little finger returns the carriage or	31	151
	carrier and spaces to the next writing line. In fact, all the typist does is	46	166
	slightly touch any key—the motor does the work. The same stroke is used	61	181
	for all keys. Typists have found that the compact keyboard helps to	75	195
	improve their skill in the touch system. The hands do not leave the	89	209
	keyboard.	91	211

4	A light touch releases the action of the tabulator key. It is not	14	225
	necessary to hold the key down until the carriage or carrier comes to a	29	240
	full stop. Keys on the electric machine require about one-fourth as much	44	255
	pressure as on the manual. The right-hand carriage return tends to	57	268
	equalize the load on the hands of the typist.	67	278

5	The electric typewriter conserves your energy, cuts costs, and	13	291
	increases production. It provides uniform print work and more and better	27	305
	carbons. Typists reach or surpass their manual speed after very little	41	319
	practice. The power at their ready command makes typists confident that	55	333
	they can type faster.	60	338

|1 |2 |3 |4 |5 |6 |7 |8 |9 |10 |11 |12 |13 |14

5.93/1.46

19-A WARMUP

Line—60 • Spacing—1 • Each Line 3 Times

WORDS

1 af ;j sf lj df kj af ;j sf lj df kj af ;j sf lj df kj af ;j   12

2 duel elan kept lake lend name nape quey them they when worm   24

3 The diver will seek the blue rocks found on the coral reef.   36

19-B INVENTORY

Tab—5 • Spacing—2 • Minutes—3 or 5

4 The goal of your study and practice is finding a good job. It is best   15
to seek employment in a field in which you think you will be interested.   30
In any event, be sure that you are qualified for the job for which you do   45
apply. Many firms list their openings in the classified section of news-   59
papers. Others fill their openings through the use of employment   73
agencies. Many employees advertise for their positions. A carefully   87
prepared ad covering the services you are prepared to offer may give you   101
a wider field from which to select when you are seeking employment.   115
If you have special skills or if you are seeking a special kind of job, you   130
will find this to be a most useful approach. There is always a demand   144
for good employees.   149

5 Your services are what you have to sell, and you should know   13 162
these as well as a good sales representative knows his or her products.   28 177
This means that you must know what you have to offer. You will do an   42 191
injustice to yourself if you overstate or understate your skills and   56 205
experience.   59 208

|1 |2 |3 |4 |5 |6 |7 |8 |9 |10 |11 |12 |13 |14   5.59/1.42

19-C SELECT PRACTICE GOAL

Base It on 19-B Writing

3 MINUTES	If your 3-minute speed is	20–29		30–39		40–49		50–59		60–69		70–up	
	And your error score is	to 6	7 up	to 5	6 up	to 4	5 up	to 3	4 up	to 2	3 up	1	2 up
	Your practice goal should be for	Sp	Ac	Sp	Ac	Sp	Ac	Sp	Ac	Sp	Ac	Sp	Ac

5 MINUTES	If your 5-minute speed is	20–29		30–39		40–49		50–59		60–69		70–up	
	And your error score is	to 7	8 up	to 6	7 up	to 5	6 up	to 4	5 up	to 3	4 up	to 2	3 up
	Your practice goal should be for	Sp	Ac	Sp	Ac	Sp	Ac	Sp	Ac	Sp	Ac	Sp	Ac

SKILL DRIVE 10

10-A   WARMUP   Line—60 • Spacing—1 • Each Line 3 Times

		WORDS
1	a;qpa;z/a; slwoslx.sl dkeidkc,dk fjrufjvmfj ghtyghbnghfjruf	12
2	bit cot cut did dug fit got hem jam key lap nap qua six vat	24
3	The mental patient mentioned dismal facts of his past life.	36

10-B   INVENTORY   Tab—5 • Spacing—2 • Minutes—3 or 5

4   An employer has every right to expect the office worker to be at   14
work on time in the morning, to lunch within the allotted time, and to   28
work until closing time. The smooth running of the office depends upon   43
strict observance of office hours. Make it a point not to be away from the   58
office during regular hours.   64

5   You will be depended upon to use your working time for business   14 78
duties and not for personal business. Your employer is paying for your   28 92
time and expects the full use of it.   36 100

6   Work out a system for your duties; do not leave matters to chance.   15 115
You will find that a tickler system, a calendar pad, and other aids will   29 129
help you promptly to do the right thing at the right time. If you have the   44 144
duty of preparing reports for a certain date, see to it that the reports are   60 160
ready by that date. You will certainly have to be dependable if it is your   75 175
duty to take care of valuables or to lock the office at night.   88 188

7   If you are dependable, you will see every task through to the finish.   15 203
You will also follow directions to the letter. You will give just as much   30 218
attention to the small task as you would to a major one. In a large office,   46 234
your small task may fit into a larger pattern. This pattern may fall to   60 248
pieces if you are not dependable.   67 255

1 2 3 4 5 6 7 8 9 10 11 12 13 14   5.33/1.34

10-C   SELECT PRACTICE GOAL   Base It on 10-B Writing

3 MINUTES	If your 3-minute speed is	20–29		30–39		40–49		50–59		60–69		70–up	
	And your error score is	to 6	7 up	to 5	6 up	to 4	5 up	to 3	4 up	to 2	3 up	1	2 up
	Your practice goal should be for	Sp	Ac	Sp	Ac	Sp	Ac	Sp	Ac	Sp	Ac	Sp	Ac

5 MINUTES	If your 5-minute speed is	20–29		30–39		40–49		50–59		60–69		70–up	
	And your error score is	to 7	8 up	to 6	7 up	to 5	6 up	to 4	5 up	to 3	4 up	to 2	3 up
	Your practice goal should be for	Sp	Ac	Sp	Ac	Sp	Ac	Sp	Ac	Sp	Ac	Sp	Ac

PROGRESS TEST 6

To measure the effectiveness of your practice in
Skill Drives 16, 17, and 18 take two 5-minute
timed writings and average your speed and error scores.

Line—60 • Tab—5 • Spacing—2

WORDS

1   Good judgment is closely allied to common sense. In practice, it   14
means that you think about what you are doing and make decisions on   28
the basis of careful thought. The use of good judgment should enter into   43
all your decisions, such as what arrangements to make, which procedure   57
to follow, which piece of equipment to recommend, or when to order   70
supplies. Of course, common sense will help you to make many of these   84
decisions; but you must always be alert to the fact that you are depending   99
upon judgment in making a choice.   106

2   Tact, discretion, and common sense are all inherent in the exercise   15   121
of good judgment. If you are tactful in dealing with complaints and in   29   135
forwarding your own ideas, you will be practicing good judgment. When-   43   149
ever a matter is left to your own discretion (and this will happen quite   58   164
often), choose your course of action carefully. Never make a judgment   72   178
unless you are willing to defend it.   80   186

3   If you give a piece of work its exact measure of importance (with   14   200
due regard to all other work before you), then you are exercising good   28   214
judgment. There will be many times when you will exercise judgment in   43   229
giving out information. If you are asked to work at the reception desk,   57   243
you will employ this trait in all your relations with callers and customers.   73   259
In human relations, good judgment will serve you well.   84   270

4   One way to improve your judgment is to discover your own faults   14   284
and weaknesses. A good rule to follow is to make certain that you have   28   298
all the facts before making a decision. If the matter is important and you   43   313
have a serious doubt about the course of action to follow, it is best to   58   328
consult others. When you are asked for advice, do not give it carelessly   73   343
without due regard to consequences because you may be called upon to   87   357
justify it. Let good common sense be your guide whenever you make a   100   370
decision.   102   372

|1 |2 |3 |4 |5 |6 |7 |8 |9 |10 |11 |12 |13 |14   5.72/1.42

10-D SPEED BUILDERS   Line—60 • Spacing—1

MOTION PRACTICE   WORDS

8 ai airy airs aims ail aids bank band bane bale balm bat bar   12
9 cl clam clan clay clap claw clew done dome doze dog dot doe   24
10 ea earn earl ears eats east easy flag flop flow foe fox for   36

RIGHT-TO-LEFT-HAND WORDS

11 late meat over odds maze last lass mats oats next mast lard   12
12 lace mass news nest mart jest jazz move need neat made java   24
13 jade left near mess left idea hope lead mere meet lava hire   36

WORD PATTERNS

14 rec recap recall record receive receipt reception recommend   12
15 tas task taste tasty tastier tasting tasteless tastefulness   24
16 hip relationship scholarship friendship township authorship   36

PHRASES AND WORDS

17 regulated reasoning majority purchase chef's waiter's quite   12
18 a good as to how a depends on of good will has a keep every   24
19 desire believe integral convince potentialities faith being   36

CONTINUITY

20 gaze daze rare laze haze maze back rack tack hack lack pace   12
21 sore bore tore core wore fore gain rain vain lain main pain   24
22 hire dire fire sire tire wire pick lick nick sick tick wick   36

INSIDE AND OUTSIDE KEYS

23 The arbor curbed the extra glints of sunshine on the table.   12
24 The texts reflected the opinion that drum tables come next.   24
25 The tiny camp was nice except for its size and so much ice.   36

$|_1 \quad |_2 \quad |_3 \quad |_4 \quad |_5 \quad |_6 \quad |_7 \quad |_8 \quad |_9 \quad |_{10} \quad |_{11} \quad |_{12}$

18-E   ACCURACY BUILDERS   Line—60 • Spacing—1

ALPHABET-REVIEW SENTENCE   WORDS

24 Even a quiet office will jump with much excitement when the   12
25 employer brings in or receives an order of record size that   24
26 involves a large stock bonus.   30

DOUBLE LETTER WORDS

27 button attaching flattened addressees attendance attempting   12
28 cutting attracted batteries connection throbbing struggling   24
29 settle batteries appointing admitting suggesting suggestion   36

WORDS AND PHRASES

30 the food late getting your customers if they do not like to   12
31 was prepared the customers will vanish there won't be sales   24
32 only vanish cooking getting prepared, customers, complaints   36

WORD PATTERNS

33 inc inch incest incense incite incision incident incomplete   12
34 ful harmful fearful wistful mindful hopeful helpful careful   24
35 ion quotation question portion mention nation motion ration   36

DOUBLE LETTER SENTENCES

36 When I finally arrived at the rally, it was partially foggy.   12
37 The peddler must paddle to the middle to address the addict.   24
38 The dirty toreador will meet the ambassador in the corridor.   36

CONCENTRATION: EACH LINE NEEDS SIX CAPITALS

39 please tell ms. dodd that mr. pitman will see her in akron.   12
40 fran saw mr. and mrs. wilhelm at the airport in des moines.   24
41 marie will go to minneapolis, san francisco, and st. louis.   36

| 1 | 2 | 3 | 4 | 5 | 6 | 7 | 8 | 9 | 10 | 11 | 12 |

This page: For speed goal, each LINE 2 times.
For accuracy goal, each GROUP 3 times.

10-E   ACCURACY BUILDERS   Line—60 • Spacing—1

ALPHABET-REVIEW SENTENCES   WORDS

26	He stretched to catch the ball before it went into a ditch.	12
27	Twenty-two of the people blocked the way into the building.	24
28	Twenty firms were competing with twice as many new outlets.	36

LEFT-TO-RIGHT-HAND WORDS

29	smoky apply spook spill annoy whip annual slyly tulip thump	12
30	slink skunk think sunny skull skill sulky shook spunk think	24
31	alumni domino comply employ skimpy skinny sloppy supply zoo	36

WORD PATTERNS

32	zed authorized baptized civilized organized utilized prized	12
33	bor bore born borax borough borrow border boredom bordering	24
34	ble able table gable hobble edible bubble arable undeniable	36

WORDS AND PHRASES

35	larger object appeal public portion thought desired require	12
36	can be a so most men and the type as well as on the all the	24
37	is to have that is and will be a great deal to prepare of a	36

CONCENTRATION

38	Please--if you can--use correct spacing. It won't be easy.	12
39	Underscore each word of two letters as soon as it is typed.	24
40	user used uses vale vase vast vats vans vary wind wine wide	36

INSIDE AND OUTSIDE KEYS

41	The old store will be open until sometime after December 8.	12
42	They all giggled too much, seemed pretty silly and foolish.	24
43	The three green hills were topped by small, leafless trees.	36

| 1 | 2 | 3 | 4 | 5 | 6 | 7 | 8 | 9 | 10 | 11 | 12 |

18-D SPEED BUILDERS   Line—60 • Spacing—1

DOUBLE LETTER WORDS   WORDS

6   accommodate assistant appearing embarrass withhold withheld   12
7   applicable beginnings commodity agreeable arrived affidavit   24
8   inner dipper hobby putty apple annum funny spoon seems week   36

WORD PATTERNS

9   pen penthouse penitentiary pennants pennyweight penal penny   12
10   nal canal paternal maternal bacchanal meridional additional   24
11   tac tachistoscope tachymeter tactician taconite tackle tack   36

PHRASES AND WORDS

12   all of us will challenge boosting assume and cutting errors   12
13   neighborhood dinner same manner was given in your an annual   24
14   group squad report command sometimes assistant organization   36

DOUBLE LETTER SENTENCES

15   An annual neighborhood dinner was given in the same manner.   12
16   I was puzzled about which embezzler had the disputed check.   24
17   Cutting errors and boosting speed will challenge all of us.   36

VOWELS

18   A stony silence covered the balcony as that ceremony ended.   12
19   Noreen's niece netted nineteen nightingales near Nashville.   24
20   Red rabbits rampaged round redundant referees responsively.   36

COMMONLY USED WORDS

21   bed boys adapted already advised advising actually addition   12
22   bill brick brief bound bonus bonds built board bulls belief   24
23   conduct charged catalog changed changing customer complying   36
     |1 |2 |3 |4 |5 |6 |7 |8 |9 |10 |11 |12

SKILL DRIVE 11

11-A WARMUP Line—60 • Spacing—1 • Each Line 3 Times

WORDS

1   a;qpa; slwosl dkeidk fjrufj ghtygh fjrufj dkeidk slwosl a;q   12

2   air cut fig ham ism jap key map nay pan rut six via wit yak   24

3   Dan, their proficient neighbor, may work the sign problems.   36

11-B INVENTORY Tab—5 • Spacing—2 • Minutes—3 or 5

4   Cleaning the type on your typewriter is a relatively simple process   15
if it is done every day. There are several methods of cleaning type. One   30
good method is to use a stiff brush. Another method is to place the   43
machine in stencil position, insert a sheet of paper or a folded facial   58
tissue into the typewriter, and then type the alphabet two or three times   73
in both lower case and capital letters. You will want to do the same for   87
the number, special character, and punctuation keys as well. Much of the   102
ink clogged in the type will then disappear. There are also many com-   116
mercial fluids to apply to the type that are fine for cleaning. As a general   132
rule, these fluids should be used often but sparingly with either a brush   147
or a cloth.   149

5   If the type is cleaned often, the typewritten work will be much   14 163
cleaner, not only on the original work but also on carbon copies and   28 177
duplicated materials. Clean type cuts a much better stencil or master   42 191
sheet, and as a result the duplicated work is much more readable. It is a   57 206
good plan to brush the type once or twice during the cutting of a stencil,   72 221
since it has been found that the type picks up matter from the stencil.   86 235

|1 |2 |3 |4 |5 |6 |7 |8 |9 |10 |11 |12 |13 |14   5.47/1.40

11-C SELECT PRACTICE GOAL Base It on 11-B Writing

3 MINUTES	If your 3-minute speed is	20–29		30–39		40–49		50–59		60–69		70–up	
	And your error score is	to 6	7 up	to 5	6 up	to 4	5 up	to 3	4 up	to 2	3 up	1	2 up
	Your practice goal should be for	Sp	Ac	Sp	Ac	Sp	Ac	Sp	Ac	Sp	Ac	Sp	Ac

5 MINUTES	If your 5-minute speed is	20–29		30–39		40–49		50–59		60–69		70–up	
	And your error score is	to 7	8 up	to 6	7 up	to 5	6 up	to 4	5 up	to 3	4 up	to 2	3 up
	Your practice goal should be for	Sp	Ac	Sp	Ac	Sp	Ac	Sp	Ac	Sp	Ac	Sp	Ac

18-A   WARMUP

Line—60 • Spacing—1 • Each Line 3 Times

		WORDS
1	fdsa jkl; fdsa jkl; fdsa jkl; fdsa jkl; fdsa jkl; fdsa jkl;	12
2	angle fight gowns handy neigh oaken queue rigor slang virus	24
3	The church choir chanted by the chapel for a city chairman.	36

18-B   INVENTORY

Tab—5 • Spacing—2 • Minutes—3 or 5

4   Your letter of application is a sales letter, and it should pave the   15
way for a job interview. A great deal of thinking should go into it. For   30
this letter you should use standard white bond paper, and it should be   44
neatly typed. The letter should be perfect even if you have to type it   58
many times to get a perfect copy. Be sure that all statements are correct.   74
It is a serious mistake to exaggerate your skills or experience. Your letter   89
should be regarded as a step toward an interview. In all cases, your letter   105
should ask for an interview. The last paragraph of the letter is the best   120
place to make this request. It is good form to address the letter to one   135
particular person. It is usually addressed to the personnel manager of a   149
firm. The tone of the letter should be sincere. The spelling and grammar   164
must be correct in all respects as this letter will be considered a sample   179
of the kind of work you will do if you are employed.   190

5   When you are granted an interview, remember that it has been   13 203
arranged to give the potential employer ideas about you as a worker. You   28 218
will want to convince the interviewer that you will be an asset to the   42 232
firm. Treat the person who interviews you with respect but not with fear.   57 247
Answer all questions honestly, and be prepared to ask a few yourself.   72 262
You will want to know the duties of the job. No one will expect you to   86 276
accept a job about which you know nothing. Be prompt, poised, and well   100 290
groomed.   102 292

| 1 | 2 | 3 | 4 | 5 | 6 | 7 | 8 | 9 | 10 | 11 | 12 | 13 | 14 | 5.49/1.39

18-C   SELECT PRACTICE GOAL

Base It on 18-B Writing

3 MINUTES	If your 3-minute speed is	20–29		30–39		40–49		50–59		60–69		70–up	
	And your error score is	to 6	7 up	to 5	6 up	to 4	5 up	to 3	4 up	to 2	3 up	1	2 up
	Your practice goal should be for	Sp	Ac	Sp	Ac	Sp	Ac	Sp	Ac	Sp	Ac	Sp	Ac

5 MINUTES	If your 5-minute speed is	20–29		30–39		40–49		50–59		60–69		70–up	
	And your error score is	to 7	8 up	to 6	7 up	to 5	6 up	to 4	5 up	to 3	4 up	to 2	3 up
	Your practice goal should be for	Sp	Ac	Sp	Ac	Sp	Ac	Sp	Ac	Sp	Ac	Sp	Ac

11-D   SPEED BUILDERS   Line—60 • Spacing—1

MOTION PRACTICE   WORDS

6   ho hop chap heap shop chip ba bay balm balk bank bank barge   12
7   ta tam talk tale tape tail ga gap gain gale game gait gases   24
8   yo you yore yogi yowl your lu lug lure luck glue land lance   36

RIGHT-TO-LEFT-HAND WORDS

9   large offer yeast octet kress kraft never press irate nerve   12
10 paved paste meter hewed hedge lever pages pacer leave heave   24
11 heart least overt otter lease hated haste later order hired   36

WORD PATTERNS

12 ern intern pattern lantern discern concern eastern northern   12
13 ele elevated electron element elected electro element elect   24
14 aze underglaze ablaze glazed blazed amazed mazed graze haze   36

PHRASES AND WORDS

15 job standard subjected controlled production high-grade and   12
16 should be need to make as a means doing a job in such a way   24
17 even scope given little charge today's agreement surprising   36

CONTINUITY

18 rare toll park mark roll pare mare moll lark hark loll hare   12
19 dare doll fare bare boll bark yell tale sock rock pale well   24
20 tell make pock lock hale jell fell gale hock dock bale bell   36

INSIDE AND OUTSIDE KEYS

21 In annexing the slums, we expect the tax table to go on up.   12
22 Cutting errors and boosting speed will challenge all of us.   24
23 Crowds of people gathered around to see what was happening.   36

| 1 | 2 | 3 | 4 | 5 | 6 | 7 | 8 | 9 | 10 | 11 | 12 |

17-E ACCURACY BUILDERS

Line—60 • Spacing—1

ALPHABET-REVIEW SENTENCE   WORDS

25 Demand for new products on the part of consumers is brought   12
26 about by quite canny job specialists who excel with zestful   24
27 skill in the advertising art.   30

DOUBLE LETTER WORDS

28 channel clipping accounted appreciate accustomed aggregated   12
29 dinners innocent approving apparently occasional announcing   24
30 annuals summons opportune accidental beginnings approaching   36

WORDS AND PHRASES

31 business is financed from of sources a number those who put   12
32 financial assumed feasible borrow insurance large portion a   24
33 the firm may wish from banks design distribution will large   36

WORD PATTERNS

34 fra frail frailty frame frantic fracture fragility fragrant   12
35 gro grog gross grope groin grocer groan grouse grout grovel   24
36 ina inane inanity inability inabsentia inaccurate inanimate   36

DOUBLE LETTER SENTENCES

37 Maxwell Miller made a million selling milk to the military.   12
38 An innocent scientist accidentally innovated the new virus.   24
39 An annual neighborhood dinner was given in the same manner.   36

CONCENTRATION: INSERT MISSING LETTERS

40 S-- w-ll n-t t-ll th-m -nl-ss - r-c--v- th- r-p-rt -n t-m-.   12
41 D--r G-org-: Pl--s- l-t u- hav- --r r-p-rt b- r-t-rn m--l.   24
42 Pl--s- sh-w m- t-- t-am sch-d-l-- -s s--n -s y-- m-k- th-m.   36
    |1 |2 |3 |4 |5 |6 |7 |8 |9 |10 |11 |12

11-E ACCURACY BUILDERS

Line—60 • Spacing—1

ALPHABET-REVIEW SENTENCES

		WORDS
24	The quarterly published in June emphasized the need for new	12
25	methods of marking examinations in various college courses.	24
26	Verna will pay lest we seize her bag of rings very quickly.	36

LEFT-TO-RIGHT-HAND WORDS

27	quill colon bloom clump gloom funny clink blink chilly bull	12
28	folio chump apply annul chill enjoy dumpy chili annoy alloy	24
29	chummy chunky chilly aloin amply amino cloy dimly bumpy don	36

WORD PATTERNS

30	but butte button butler butcher buttery butterfly buttercup	12
31	ink link mink pink rink sink clink think blink drink shrink	24
32	jou jounce journal journey journalism journalize journalist	36

WORDS AND PHRASES

33	accomplish necessary helpful toward bounce flash sharp aims	12
34	to your should be of the seems to of it if very is the most	24
35	popping untangling instead prevent collide bars case appear	36

CONCENTRATION

36	dark bark hark lark mark park line nine dine fine vine wine	12
37	jolt molt colt volt bolt dolt hour pour dour four tour sour	24
38	Radical researchers ransack rulings ruthlessly and rapidly.	36

INSIDE AND OUTSIDE KEYS

39	Responsible leaders usually worry about what they tell you.	12
40	Important persons will receive credit when they ask for it.	24
41	Elementary factors usually concern things basic for us all.	36

| 1 | 2 | 3 | 4 | 5 | 6 | 7 | 8 | 9 | 10 | 11 | 12 |

17-D   SPEED BUILDERS   Line—60 • Spacing—1

DOUBLE LETTER WORDS   WORDS

7   wood roof room moon mood look hook cool door cook boot boom   12
8   commend accounts accompany accessible accumulate accomplish   24
9   little three hopped willows creek office meeting small will   36

WORD PATTERNS

10 act activate activity actuality actuary actuation actuaries   12
11 ly helpfully shrewdly likely lately firmly finely apply sly   24
12 fla flammable flashiness flashlight flatcar flaky flag flat   36

PHRASES AND WORDS

13 three deer of the hopped out the willows into the creek and   12
14 our meeting too small will be the hall office down dazzling   24
15 foolproof way our books for keeping the bookkeepers flowers   36

DOUBLE LETTER SENTENCES

16 Three little deer hopped out of the willows into the creek.   12
17 The office down the hall will be too small for our meeting.   24
18 The bookkeepers need a foolproof way for keeping our books.   36

VOWELS

19 The old owl flew over and landed on the onion with an odor.   12
20 She and another amiable acquaintance anxiously await Act V.   24
21 Nine navigators nicely nailed ninety nails near New Jersey.   36

COMMONLY USED WORDS

22 cars committee commission connection collection certificate   12
23 beg begin boards bother bureau branch bottle booked bundles   24
24 acts among American attached agreement advisable appreciate   36

|1 |2 |3 |4 |5 |6 |7 |8 |9 |10 |11 |12

12-A   WARMUP

Line—60 • Spacing—1 • Each Line 3 Times

WORDS

1   a;z/a; slx.sl dkc,dk fjvmfj ghbngh fjvmfj dkc,dk slx.sl a;z   12

2   hand lake pair pale pens sick sigh when wide wish with work   24

3   The heirs to the estate were happy about the ladies' health.   36

12-B   INVENTORY

Tab—5 • Spacing—2 • Minutes—3 or 5

4   The business world is always looking for more effective ways of   14
operating. Often you may have to adapt yourself to new equipment. If you   29
do this to the best of your ability, you will soon be the master of it. You   44
must be prepared to progress with your company and to adapt your skill   58
to its needs. You are expected to respond readily to changing conditions   73
and to adjust quickly to new situations so that the work may go on   87
smoothly. There will be instances when you will be called upon to do   101
work that you dislike or to follow a new procedure in getting out a   114
report. The willingness you show to adapt yourself to these changes may   129
mean a step toward promotion.   135

5   If you prove yourself to be a person who adapts easily to changing   14   149
conditions and new situations, your chances for promotion will be greatly   29   164
increased. There will be instances when you are given tasks that you   43   178
dislike. The way in which you adapt yourself to these tasks will make   57   192
them easy or difficult. There will also be instances when you will have to   73   208
work under pressure of time. If you remain calm and do the job to the   87   222
best of your ability, you will prove yourself adaptable. If you develop this 102 237
trait and practice it, you increase your chances for success in the business 118 253
world. So be prepared to adapt yourself and your typing skill to the   132 267
needs of the company for which you work. Be prepared to progress with   146 281
your company and to adapt yourself to changing procedures.   158 293

|1 |2 |3 |4 |5 |6 |7 |8 |9 |10 |11 |12 |13 |14   5.57/1.41

12-C   SELECT PRACTICE GOAL

Base It on 12-B Writing

3 MINUTES	If your 3-minute speed is	20–29		30–39		40–49		50–59		60–69		70–up	
	And your error score is	to 6	7 up	to 5	6 up	to 4	5 up	to 3	4 up	to 2	3 up	1	2 up
	Your practice goal should be for	Sp	Ac	Sp	Ac	Sp	Ac	Sp	Ac	Sp	Ac	Sp	Ac

5 MINUTES	If your 5-minute speed is	20–29		30–39		40–49		50–59		60–69		70–up	
	And your error score is	to 7	8 up	to 6	7 up	to 5	6 up	to 4	5 up	to 3	4 up	to 2	3 up
	Your practice goal should be for	Sp	Ac	Sp	Ac	Sp	Ac	Sp	Ac	Sp	Ac	Sp	Ac

17-A WARMUP

Line—60 • Spacing—1 • Each Line 3 Times

WORDS

1 ce ce cede cere celt cell cent mo mo mow mop moss move moles   12

2 ra ra rat raps raid rate race im im imp imbed imbues imports   24

3 sa sa sat saps said saws same un un unto unify unfit untwist   36

17-B INVENTORY

Tab—5 • Spacing—2 • Minutes—3 or 5

4   An employer can be proud of the secretarial workers in an office   14
when correspondence is typed in mailable condition. This not only   27
indicates that the office employees are typing rather well but also may   42
reveal that the typists are doing a very good job when checking their   56
work for each day.   60

5   Two of the traits accurate typists possess that permit them to do   14 74
such a good job of proofreading are especially important. Good typists   29 89
are more than likely good spellers. If they do not have problems with   43 103
spelling, they will finish a task in less time because they don't have to   58 118
waste their effort looking for words in the dictionary before they can   72 132
start to type.   75 135

6   Good typists also know the basics of punctuation. An employer   13 148
seldom refers to punctuation during dictation and expects the secretary   27 162
to insert all punctuation marks that are needed when typing the final   41 176
copy. The willingness of a good typist to take care of the punctuation   55 190
details in a letter will pay off at some later date, because the correctness   71 206
of the work will soon be well known.   78 213

|1 |2 |3 |4 |5 |6 |7 |8 |9 |10 |11 |12 |13 |14   5.82/1.51

17-C SELECT PRACTICE GOAL

Base It on 17-B Writing

3 MINUTES	If your 3-minute speed is	20–29		30–39		40–49		50–59		60–69		70–up	
	And your error score is	to 6	7 up	to 5	6 up	to 4	5 up	to 3	4 up	to 2	3 up	1	2 up
	Your practice goal should be for	Sp	Ac	Sp	Ac	Sp	Ac	Sp	Ac	Sp	Ac	Sp	Ac

5 MINUTES	If your 5-minute speed is	20–29		30–39		40–49		50–59		60–69		70–up	
	And your error score is	to 7	8 up	to 6	7 up	to 5	6 up	to 4	5 up	to 3	4 up	to 2	3 up
	Your practice goal should be for	Sp	Ac	Sp	Ac	Sp	Ac	Sp	Ac	Sp	Ac	Sp	Ac

12-D SPEED BUILDERS   Line—60 • Spacing—1

MOTION PRACTICE

		WORDS
6	py spy spry pays prey spryly ag ages flag snag page lags ag	12
7	ly lay lyre clay ally sorely at ants atom flat that slat at	24
8	yo you youth young younger youngish youngster yourselves yo	36

RIGHT-TO-LEFT-HAND WORDS

9	ice jar jaw jet hat how his hid hex hew her haw hag had lad	12
10	head hear heat heed herb here herd hers hare hard hate have	24
11	oat odd ore pad par pat pea lay leg let mar mat net new use	36

WORD PATTERNS

12	suc succumb succeed suction success succotash succulent suc	12
13	fou foul four found fount fought foundry founder founderous	24
14	ext extol extant extent extend extract exterior extortioner	36

PHRASES AND WORDS

15	are same bored results nothing message equipped transaction	12
16	that goes made a to get up at once of each with no time the	24
17	require cardboard one method already instead written judged	36

CONTINUITY

18	airy ally alto alum bade bail bait bald calf calk calm camp	12
19	dais damp dark data earn east echo eddy face fade fair fake	24
20	gait gale gall gang hair hale half hall ibex ibis idea idle	36

INSIDE AND OUTSIDE KEYS

21	These comical creatures offer an amusing touch of nonsense.	12
22	The success will show them all that effort really pays off.	24
23	The bookkeepers need a foolproof way for keeping the books.	36

|1 |2 |3 |4 |5 |6 |7 |8 |9 |10 |11 |12

16-E   ACCURACY BUILDERS   Line—60 • Spacing—1

ALPHABET-REVIEW SENTENCE   WORDS

26	Ease of expansion, limited liability, and larger size ought	12
27	to be just qualitative advantages which were often taken as	24
28	reasons for a corporate form.	30

DOUBLE LETTER WORDS

29	assured essential equipping occupying suggestive aggressive	12
30	arrange affected erroneous permitting connecting immaterial	24
31	winning assistant addressee following collecting sufficient	36

WORDS AND PHRASES

32	never asked the unlabeled to photograph box of phosphate to	12
33	recommended reclaiming records will recall scholarship will	24
34	acquaintance acquitted acquiring bad acquisition work asked	36

WORD PATTERNS

35	doc dock docile docket doctrine docility doctrinal document	12
36	dra drain drafty drama drape dramatic drastic dragnet draft	24
37	amb amber amble ambition ambush ambulate ambitious ambulant	36

DOUBLE LETTER SENTENCES

38	The office down the hall will be too small for our meeting.	12
39	The vacuum nullified the sudden hubbub from my upper study.	24
40	I was puzzled about which embezzler had the disputed check.	36

CONCENTRATION: EACH LINE NEEDS SIX CAPITALS

41	ms. jolson got a new ford last friday in detroit, michigan.	12
42	j. r. everett's full name is said to be john ralph everett.	24
43	hank rode the "sunshine special" from chicago to st. louis.	36

|₁ |₂ |₃ |₄ |₅ |₆ |₇ |₈ |₉ |₁₀ |₁₁ |₁₂

12-E ACCURACY BUILDERS   Line—60 • Spacing—1

ALPHABET-REVIEW SENTENCES   WORDS

24 The law makes all juvenile delinquents, except those in the   12
25 company of their parents, avoid such organizations as this.   24
26 The completion of the math building was a monumental event.   36

LEFT-TO-RIGHT-HAND WORDS

27 calm call chip copy cool cook coin coil clip chum chop chap   12
28 dunk film foil folk flop gill gulp dump dull doom doll dill   24
29 buoy bunk ball bulk boon boom book boll boil ally ahoy bill   36

WORD PATTERNS

30 urn turn burn spurn return churned adjourn sojourn returned   12
31 cou coupe couple cousin court county country coupon counter   24
32 sub subtle suburb submit sublet sublime subscribe subdivide   36

WORDS AND PHRASES

33 thoughtful efficiency practice emphasis definite judge work   12
34 into the that a who come turned to and my of my own my home   24
35 politeness interesting fireplace associate business develop   36

CONCENTRATION

36 Experts frequently say that work on alphabetic sentences is   12
37 judged a good way, a prize way, to improve typing accuracy.   24
38 House plants need plenty of sunshine to be strong and tall.   36

INSIDE AND OUTSIDE KEYS

39 He was irresponsible, irrational, and irritating to my pal.   12
40 She showed the king a newly written score for the symphony.   24
41 The aid by the big man kept the new land for the city lake.   36

|1 |2 |3 |4 |5 |6 |7 |8 |9 |10 |11 |12

16-D SPEED BUILDERS

Line—60 • Spacing—1

DOUBLE LETTER WORDS

WORDS

8 speedily squeezed letters sixteen fifteen padded seemed too   12
9 basketball sessions attend fellows three tall will hill all   24
10 differences dummy cannot assets dinner pitted tell well add   36

WORD PATTERNS

11 wor workmanship worriment worthwhile workman worker worship   12
12 ant anticipation antagonize antenna anterior anthem antique   24
13 sec secretaries seclusion secession section security sector   36

PHRASES AND WORDS

14 that launch buyers success chance service examine recognize   12
15 is profit private exactly feature prospering accomplishment   24
16 to get shown price public willing because product expensive   36

DOUBLE LETTER SENTENCES

17 Bill speedily squeezed sixteen letters into fifteen spaces.   12
18 All the tall fellows will attend three basketball sessions.   24
19 Larry cannot tell too well the differences in dummy assets.   36

VOWELS

20 Many mornings my mother makes magnificent muffins and milk.   12
21 Eccentric engineers exert efforts in elementary enterprise.   24
22 Ike insulted Inez's intelligence inviting Iris ice skating.   36

COMMONLY USED WORDS

23 carry convenience considerable consideration correspondence   12
24 bulk booklet biggest bringing belonging bulletins beginning   24
25 advise adapted apparently absolutely accordance accordingly   36

1 2 3 4 5 6 7 8 9 10 11 12

PROGRESS TEST 4

To measure the effectiveness of your practice in Skill Drives 10, 11, and 12 take two 5-minute timed writings and average your speed and error scores.

Line—60 • Tab—5 • Spacing—2

WORDS

1	Make sure that what you type is correct and in good form before you	15
	let it go out. Do not be careless in your proofreading. It includes more	30
	than just finding errors in typing. You should check closely for errors in	45
	grammar, use of the hyphen, word usage, placement, and correct style. An	60
	error in copying may mean a serious change in the meaning of words or	74
	amounts in figures. For example, if you put a decimal point in the wrong	88
	place, it may mean an error of a large sum. If you leave out a comma, it	103
	may change the meaning of the sentence or leave a doubt about the	116
	meaning intended. A good typist will check each letter, figure, punctua-	131
	tion mark, and space. If you type words that are not familiar, make it a	146
	rule to check the spelling and correct usage. It is not expected that you	161
	will type without making any errors, but an employer will consider it a	175
	very serious matter if you fail to see and correct your errors.	188

2	If you use the paper-bail method of proofreading, it will help you	14	202
	to follow the line of writing since the platen is turned until the paper	29	217
	bail is just below each line of writing. If the paper is out of the machine,	45	233
	a ruler or a piece of colored paper or cardboard may be used in place of	59	247
	the paper bail. If the work is very important or contains many figures, it	74	262
	is best to have two people proofread it. The spelling of names and figures	90	278
	should be double-checked. A good way to proofread lists of any type is to	105	293
	count the number of items in each list and then check item by item with	119	307
	the copy.	121	309

3	Many typists check each page before taking it out of the machine.	14	323
	In this way time is saved in correcting errors, as good alignment is main-	29	338
	tained. Make your erasures in the proper way on all copies. The typing	44	353
	job is complete only when you have proofread what you have typed. Read	58	367
	slowly—not word for word—but letter for letter. At all times, you should	73	382
	aim for correctness rather than speed.	81	390

| 1 | 2 | 3 | 4 | 5 | 6 | 7 | 8 | 9 | 10 | 11 | 12 | 13 | 14 | 5.23/1.34 |

PROGRESS TEST 4　　　　　　　　　　　　　　　　　　　　**40**

16-A   WARMUP   Line—60 • Spacing—1 • Each Line 3 Times

WORDS

1   fgfdsa jhjkl; fgfdsa jhjkl; fgfdsa jhjkl; fgfdsa jhjkl; fgf   12
2   div ivy rov via vic vid vie vir vis vit vor vos vow vug voe   24
3   To blend both vogue and quantity, they cut ivy for the urn.   36

16-B   INVENTORY   Tab—5 • Spacing—2 • Minutes—3 or 5

4   Make it a point to learn the reference sources in your office, and   14
you will soon be able to find facts in a hurry. You may be called upon to   29
furnish information when there is no time to waste. This does not mean   44
that you will be expected to know all the answers, but it does mean that   58
you should be able to find the desired data quickly. Keep the books you   73
use often close at hand.   78

5   You should know how to make the best use of the dictionary and   14   92
the telephone book. Every typist must know how to use a dictionary   27   105
correctly. Often you will have to use this book to check the spelling or   42   120
exact meaning of a word. It is also useful for word division. If you have   57   135
any doubt about words, use the dictionary without fail.   69   147

6   When you are checking for addresses, it is often best to use the   14   161
telephone book. Learn how to make proper use of the classified section of   29   176
the telephone book. It contains lists of dealers and their products as well   44   191
as lists of firms under the services they offer. Correct use of these   59   206
reference books will save you much time.   67   214

7   If you have to ask someone for help in locating information, state   14   228
your problem clearly so that there is no doubt about the object of your   29   243
search. Do not depend upon your memory, but make a note of the   42   256
information that is desired. In each case be sure that you know exactly   56   270
what you are looking for.   61   275

|1 |2 |3 |4 |5 |6 |7 |8 |9 |10 |11 |12 |13 |14   5.39/1.35

16-C   SELECT PRACTICE GOAL   **Base It on 16-B Writing**

3 MINUTES	If your 3-minute speed is	20–29		30–39		40–49		50–59		60–69		70–up	
	And your error score is	to 6	7 up	to 5	6 up	to 4	5 up	to 3	4 up	to 2	3 up	1	2 up
	Your practice goal should be for	Sp	Ac	Sp	Ac	Sp	Ac	Sp	Ac	Sp	Ac	Sp	Ac

5 MINUTES	If your 5-minute speed is	20–29		30–39		40–49		50–59		60–69		70–up	
	And your error score is	to 7	8 up	to 6	7 up	to 5	6 up	to 4	5 up	to 3	4 up	to 2	3 up
	Your practice goal should be for	Sp	Ac	Sp	Ac	Sp	Ac	Sp	Ac	Sp	Ac	Sp	Ac

13-A   WARMUP
Line—60 • Spacing—1 • Each Line 3 Times

WORDS

1   fa j; fs jl fd jk fa j; fs jl fd jk fa j; fs jl fd jk fa j;   12

2   aisle angle bogus eight field dandy rifle shake shelf signs   24

3   The two towns had formal fights to get the few forms fixed.   36

13-B   INVENTORY
Tab—5 • Spacing—2 • Minutes—3 or 5

4   The top of a desk is intended for one purpose only—a place to   14
work. Do not clutter your desk top with papers, folders, paper clips, trays,   29
or odds and ends. There is a logical location for every article that you   44
use. Do not make a supply center out of your desk top. If you give a   58
little thought to working out a convenient arrangement of materials to   72
meet your own needs, you will never have to search for supplies. Good   87
order will save you time and effort.   94

5   The top right-hand drawer is the most convenient to use for   13 107
stationery. You should arrange letterheads, carbon paper, and second   27 121
sheets in the slanting pockets (if available) of this drawer in the order in   42 136
which they are used in making up carbon packs. Place envelopes either   56 150
at the front or the side of the drawer. The next drawer should be used   71 165
for supplies, such as paper clips, ruler, pencils, and erasers. It is best to   87 181
arrange these articles in trays or boxes so that they may easily be found.   102 196
The articles used most often should be placed nearest the front of the   116 210
drawer. The third drawer should be used for work in progress, the tickler   131 225
file, and other frequently needed materials.   140 234

6   Keep the office reference books that are used most often on the top   15 249
of your desk or within easy reach. File trays for incoming and outgoing   29 263
work should be placed within easy reach too. Be sure to keep a pad and   44 278
pencil near the phone. The size and type of desk govern the arrangement   58 292
of these things to a great extent.   65 299

| 1 | 2 | 3 | 4 | 5 | 6 | 7 | 8 | 9 | 10 | 11 | 12 | 13 | 14 |

5.54/1.36

13-C   SELECT PRACTICE GOAL
Base It on 13-B Writing

3 MINUTES	If your 3-minute speed is	20–29		30–39		40–49		50–59		60–69		70–up	
	And your error score is	to 6	7 up	to 5	6 up	to 4	5 up	to 3	4 up	to 2	3 up	1	2 up
	Your practice goal should be for	Sp	Ac	Sp	Ac	Sp	Ac	Sp	Ac	Sp	Ac	Sp	Ac

5 MINUTES	If your 5-minute speed is	20–29		30–39		40–49		50–59		60–69		70–up	
	And your error score is	to 7	8 up	to 6	7 up	to 5	6 up	to 4	5 up	to 3	4 up	to 2	3 up
	Your practice goal should be for	Sp	Ac	Sp	Ac	Sp	Ac	Sp	Ac	Sp	Ac	Sp	Ac

To measure the effectiveness of your practice in
Skill Drives 13, 14, and 15 take two 5-minute
timed writings and average your speed and error scores.

Line—60 • Tab—5 • Spacing—2

WORDS

1   The wishes of your employer should govern your procedure for   **13**
receiving callers. If there is any doubt, find out whether your employer   **28**
wants to see the caller. If not, use tact, and try to help the caller in any   **44**
way that you can. Your treatment of callers can create goodwill for your   **58**
firm. People who visit the office should be received on a friendly but   **73**
impersonal basis.   **77**

2   You should keep a list of the appointments for the day. You should   **15** **92**
announce a person who has an appointment as soon as he or she arrives.   **29** **106**
If you find out that your employer cannot keep an appointment, make   **43** **120**
every effort to postpone or cancel it before the caller arrives at the office.   **59** **136**

3   Insist on getting the name and business of each caller. Most callers   **15** **151**
are easy to greet, but a few are troublesome. It is here that you will need   **30** **166**
tact and firmness. In a sense, you are acting as office host or hostess;   **45** **181**
but you are also the guard of your employer's time. You should keep a   **59** **195**
complete record of the calls you handle each day. List the name,   **73** **209**
business, and purpose of each visitor in a notebook or in a card file.   **87** **223**
Any data that you may be able to obtain about the person who is calling   **101** **237**
will be useful.   **104** **241**

4   Remember that many office jobs call for meeting the public at close   **15** **256**
range, and it is important that tact and courtesy be exercised. What you   **29** **270**
say and do will reflect upon your firm. Give a personal greeting when-   **44** **285**
ever you can. The ability to remember names and faces is a trait which   **58** **299**
will help you on the job.   **63** **304**

5   You should know where your employer is and when he or she is   **13** **317**
expected back. A thorough knowledge of the setup of the office and the   **28** **332**
duties of the workers is essential. Be alert, tactful, friendly, and well-   **43** **347**
groomed at all times. Treat people with your best attention.   **55** **359**

|1 |2 |3 |4 |5 |6 |7 |8 |9 |10 |11 |12 |13 |14   5.52/1.37

13-D   SPEED BUILDERS   Line—60 • Spacing—1

MOTION STUDY: LETTERS AND WORDS   WORDS

7 to to tam talk tale tape tail hp hp hap chap heap shop chip   12
8 ga ga gap gain gale game gait yo yo you yore yogi yowl your   24
9 ce ce ice nice mice lace pace ny ny any tiny many zany deny   36

LOCATIONAL SECURITY SENTENCES

10 Oftentimes people need to give a little more of themselves.   12
11 Since this is autumn, we will be having a frost quite soon.   24
12 The new African violet bloomed for two weeks and then died.   36

WORD PATTERNS

13 pho phonics phobia phony phonology photochemical photoflash   12
14 non none nonfat noncredit noncoloric nonentity noncommittal   24
15 hea head heat heater hearse heart health heartier headfirst   36

STROKING: DOWNHILL SENTENCES

16 National remedies attain little where local ones work well.   12
17 Quantitative problems engage things other than what you do.   24
18 Neighborhood visitors praise their good work with that boy.   36

PHRASES AND WORDS

19 and his can go to the and buy are challenges efficient work   12
20 simultaneously emphasize inaccuracy rearranging tutored for   24
21 for the show that you will you will to make the between the   36

MOTION STUDY: SECOND- AND THIRD-ROW STROKES

22 Tell all the people who say that you are good for the task.   12
23 A show will take a lot of work if we are to write to folks.   24
24 We should use a high quality of paper if we wish good work.   36

|1 |2 |3 |4 |5 |6 |7 |8 |9 |10 |11 |12

15-E ACCURACY BUILDERS   Line—60 • Spacing—1

LOCATIONAL SECURITY DRILL   WORDS

25 vex wig yon vie woe yank zero vice wood yawn zither voluble 12
26 zzaz zzez zziz zzoz zzuz zzaz zzez zziz zzoz zzuz zzaz zzez 24
27 zed zip zoo zee zip zone zany zeal zinc zoom zealot zoology 36

STEADYING WRISTS

28 I cheerily said that we can't and won't abandon the abacus. 12
20 Print your name and your address on your subscription book. 24
30 In fact, I saw a deer get in a cart and start on my onions. 36

WORD PATTERNS

31 exp expand expect expanse expedite expelled expense explode 12
32 cor cord coral cordial corelate coronary corporal corporate 24
33 ana anatomy analogies analogous analogize anachronic analog 36

CONCENTRATION: SPELL WORDS FULLY AND CORRECTLY

34 Deer Frnak: Wee shal bee veree plezd too se yu next mumth. 12
35 The saels gruop hoeps that teh delivrey mya arirve ni time. 24
36 The preemum rait 4 that policee wil goe up at aige sevunty. 36

WORDS AND PHRASES

37 about the antique urn neighbor about it and if he has ideas 12
38 big less accept exacting anything appropriate qualification 24
39 can answer about the and pay who has the warrant accept the 36

MOTION STUDY: SENTENCE DRILL

40 The interviewer can answer the questions about the warrant. 12
41 The widow with the worn antique urn is the island neighbor. 24
42 We were welcome when Pam showed the manager Woodrow's card. 36

    |1 |2 |3 |4 |5 |6 |7 |8 |9 |10 |11 |12

This page: For speed goal, each LINE 2 times.
For accuracy goal, each GROUP 3 times.

13-E ACCURACY BUILDERS

Line—60 • Spacing—1

LOCATIONAL SECURITY DRILL WORDS

25 vvav wwew yyiy zzoz vvuv wwaw yyey zziz vvov wwuw yyay zzez 12
26 yyay yyey yyiy yyoy yyuy yyay yyey yyiy yyoy yyuy yyay yyey 24
27 zzaz zzez zziz zzoz zzuz zzaz zzez zziz zzoz zzuz zzaz zzez 36

STEADYING WRISTS

28 That professor is very hard, but everyone learns something. 12
29 Education is a facet of your life which you should cherish. 24
30 These sweet designs feature bright, fluttering butterflies. 36

WORD PATTERNS

31 imm immature immediate immense immerge immerse immovability 12
32 irr irresponsive irradiate irradiator irrational irrelative 24
33 hun hunt hung hunk hunch hunts hunger hunted hungry hundred 36

CONCENTRATION: INSERT MISSING LETTERS

34 My cousin could make --- suit out of corduroy --- our aunt. 12
35 Wh-n sh--ld - b- -bl- t- -xp-ct t- h--r fr-m th- -th-r b-y? 24
36 The kid borrowed money in --- corridor for --- horror show. 36

WORDS AND PHRASES

37 fastest evening learned sport splits matter has lost at won 12
38 at all he may at the at our told us can be in only a to the 24
39 politeness interesting fireplace business associate develop 36

MOTION STUDY: SENTENCE DRILL

40 Jan must find some help if Joe is to work for the new firm. 12
41 One or two of the men say that they must be paid right now. 24
42 We will do all we can to pay them for what they do for her. 36

|1 |2 |3 |4 |5 |6 |7 |8 |9 |10 |11 |12

15-D SPEED BUILDERS   Line—60 • Spacing—1

MOTION STUDY: LETTERS AND WORDS   WORDS

7   an aye auto airy audit ambush burner bowls busy born bud by   12
8   co cot city coal chair chapel dismal divot dish duck due do   24
9   el eye envy elan eight enamel formal flake form fish for fy   36

LOCATIONAL SECURITY SENTENCES

10   This is one of the rocks that they found down by the docks.   12
11   It is an old shirt, but a warm one, that fits me very well.   24
12   It is a good thing to be able to laugh when one is serious.   36

WORD PATTERNS

13   mas mass mash mask mast master mastic masque massage massif   12
14   mal male mall malcontent malfunction mallet mallard malodor   24
15   ing doing being tying seeing asking begging telling singing   36

STROKING: DOWNHILL SENTENCES

16   The first thing the new men must do is to work on the dock.   12
17   We knew it would rain, and rain it did in that second half.   24
18   The tour is a long one that will let us see the old sights.   36

PHRASES AND WORDS

19   consistently position expert growth bounce reason stay same   12
20   important correctly framework wrist elbows travel body just   24
21   confidence tutored without finger course strike steps sound   36

MOTION STUDY: SECOND- AND THIRD-ROW KEYS

22   It would please these boys to see the poetry typed so well.   12
23   They told us that he would try to ship the order this week.   24
24   She may be or she may not be the girl who told us about it.   36

14-A   WARMUP   Line—60 • Spacing—1 • Each Line 3 Times

WORDS

1   af;jsfljdfkjaf;j af;jsfljdfkjaf;j af;jsfljdfkjaf;j af;jsflj   12

2   aid bit cut doe eye for got hem icy jam key lap men nap owl   24

3   The peddler can paddle to the middle to address the addict.   36

14-B   INVENTORY   Tab—5 • Spacing—2 • Minutes—3 or 5

4   It is wise to follow a definite plan when practicing if you wish to   15
obtain the best results. Make it a policy to practice every day. Forty to   30
sixty minutes of practice a day for five days will be of more value to you   45
than five continuous hours in one day. Too long a period of practice at   59
any one time will create fatigue. Do not practice when you are tired, for   74
you will develop a lack of control and make many errors.   86

5   You need to have a definite aim when you practice. If you practice   15   101
with a specific purpose in mind, you will have more success in im-   28   114
proving your skill. Alphabetic drills are useful as practice; they should be   43   129
typed for control rather than for speed. An alphabetic drill should be   58   144
typed at least three times in a row or until you can type the more   71   157
difficult words and phrases in it with ease.   80   166

6   Warmup drills can be a great aid to you if used for a definite   14   180
purpose. You can better your stroking rate by typing one of these drills a   29   195
few times before timed writings. This limbers up your fingers and gives   43   209
you more control and better rhythm. The first line must be typed slowly,   58   224
the second line faster, and the last line as fast as you can without losing   73   239
control of your rhythm.   78   244

|₁ |₂ |₃ |₄ |₅ |₆ |₇ |₈ |₉ |₁₀ |₁₁ |₁₂ |₁₃ |₁₄   5.37/1.38

14-C   SELECT PRACTICE GOAL   Base It on 14-B Writing

3 MINUTES	If your 3-minute speed is	20–29		30–39		40–49		50–59		60–69		70–up	
	And your error score is	to 6	7 up	to 5	6 up	to 4	5 up	to 3	4 up	to 2	3 up	1	2 up
	Your practice goal should be for	Sp	Ac	Sp	Ac	Sp	Ac	Sp	Ac	Sp	Ac	Sp	Ac

5 MINUTES	If your 5-minute speed is	20–29		30–39		40–49		50–59		60–69		70–up	
	And your error score is	to 7	8 up	to 6	7 up	to 5	6 up	to 4	5 up	to 3	4 up	to 2	3 up
	Your practice goal should be for	Sp	Ac	Sp	Ac	Sp	Ac	Sp	Ac	Sp	Ac	Sp	Ac

15-A   WARMUP   Line—60 • Spacing—1 • Each Line 3 Times

WORDS

1   nan nbn ncn ndn nen nfn ngn nhn nin njn nkn nln nmn non npn   12

2   bear cart cage dart feat hill kill lily mill nook pink west   24

3   The lack of jobs in the mining region caused men hardships.   36

15-B   INVENTORY   Tab—5 • Spacing—2 • Minutes—3 or 5

4   　　　Make it a policy to answer your phone promptly. On the phone,   14
you represent your company, and you will want to reflect credit upon   27
both the firm and yourself. Learn the correct procedure for handling   41
phone calls in your office. Be courteous and helpful. Your voice is the   56
direct contact between your firm and the person on the other end of the   70
line. It is important that you speak naturally and at a normal rate on the   86
phone. Be concise, but not curt. Courtesy is the keystone of good tele-   100
phone procedure.   104

5   　　　A long delay in answering your phone gives a bad impression.   13   117
When you answer the phone, be sure to have pencil and paper handy to   27   131
write down the message. Most firms have message forms on which this is   42   146
done. Get the message correct, and make sure that it reaches the proper   56   160
person. You will often receive requests for information over the phone. If   72   176
you have to look up the information, make it clear to the caller whether   86   190
he or she should remain on the line, call back, or wait for you to call   100   204
back.   102   206

6   　　　In a large firm, you are likely to receive calls that can be answered   15   221
only by someone else. Inform the calling party that you must transfer the   30   236
call to another person, and then transfer it promptly to the correct person   45   251
or place. Speak directly into the phone. Cultivate a good telephone voice,   61   267
and remember you are speaking for the firm. Try to help, and never fail   75   281
to be courteous.   78   284

|1　|2　|3　|4　|5　|6　|7　|8　|9　|10　|11　|12　|13　|14   5.57/1.40

15-C   SELECT PRACTICE GOAL   Base It on 15-B Writing

3 MINUTES	If your 3-minute speed is	20–29		30–39		40–49		50–59		60–69		70–up	
	And your error score is	to 6	7 up	to 5	6 up	to 4	5 up	to 3	4 up	to 2	3 up	1	2 up
	Your practice goal should be for	Sp	Ac	Sp	Ac	Sp	Ac	Sp	Ac	Sp	Ac	Sp	Ac

5 MINUTES	If your 5-minute speed is	20–29		30–39		40–49		50–59		60–69		70–up	
	And your error score is	to 7	8 up	to 6	7 up	to 5	6 up	to 4	5 up	to 3	4 up	to 2	3 up
	Your practice goal should be for	Sp	Ac	Sp	Ac	Sp	Ac	Sp	Ac	Sp	Ac	Sp	Ac

14-D SPEED BUILDERS   Line—60 • Spacing—1

MOTION STUDY: LETTERS AND WORDS   WORDS

7	up up cup soup coup sups cups ba ba bay balm balk band bank	12
8	on on son song bone gone bond ex ex vex next text flex ibex	24
9	in in tin find fine tint wink tb tb tab tabs stub stab tubs	36

LOCATIONAL SECURITY SENTENCES

10	It is not right to turn down the work when it pays so well.	12
11	They said that they would do what they said they should do.	24
12	They may say this is so, or they may say that it is not so.	36

WORD PATTERNS

13	qua quack quaint quarrel quarter quadrant quadrangle quarry	12
14	car carat carrot carbon carbine carcass carnival carburetor	24
15	off offer offend office offset official officiate officious	36

STROKING: DOWNHILL SENTENCES

16	Qualified experts thought the final work loads were better.	12
17	Delivery problems prevent filling orders from Esther or me.	24
18	Responsible leaders usually worry about what they tell you.	36

PHRASES AND WORDS

19	in a day's in their the two was about while she of the work	12
20	get her work at for her desk when she would in this way and	24
21	beat pools while nature filing routine specialist organized	36

MOTION STUDY: UPPER AND LOWER KEYS

22	The efficient secretary regards many duties as a challenge.	12
23	Pam and Bo played ball all afternoon until they grew tired.	24
24	The members of my new class offer newer, interesting ideas.	36

|1 |2 |3 |4 |5 |6 |7 |8 |9 |10 |11 |12

14-E   ACCURACY BUILDERS   Line—60 • Spacing—1

LOCATIONAL SECURITY DRILL   WORDS

25   wwaw wwew wwiw wwow wwuw wwaw wwew wwiw wwow wwuw wwaw wwew   12

26   vvav wwew yyiy zzoz vvuv wwaw yyey zziz vvov wwuw yyay zzez   24

27   war wet win won was well wide wool wash weed window worsted   36

STEADYING WRISTS

28   The bookkeepers need a foolproof way for keeping the books.   12

29   They all giggled too much--seemed pretty silly and foolish.   24

30   The office down the hall will be too small for our meeting.   36

WORD PATTERNS

31   sup super superb supper superior superman superjet supplant   12

32   dis disable disagree disallow disaster disbelieve discovery   24

33   exc excel excess excise excite exceed exclamatory excellent   36

CONCENTRATION: TYPE EACH LINE AS IT SAYS

34   After typing this sentence underscore words that have an E.   12

35   Please --if you can--usecorrect spacing. It won 't beeasy.   24

36   Capitalize each word of four letters as soon as it's typed.   36

WORDS AND PHRASES

37   each night dusk breath of cool air swept down into the hill   12

38   report success has gone to equip should be promoted classes   24

39   of the was stolen from the cab quite chef's beware majority   36

MOTION STUDY: SENTENCE DRILL

40   Each night at dusk a breath of cool air swept down into the   12

41   city from the distant hills. Each night at dusk this fresh   24

42   life flowed to the city to stir up its heart and its pulse.   36
     |1 |2 |3 |4 |5 |6 |7 |8 |9 |10 |11 |12